Order this book online at www.trafford.com/08-1152
or email orders@trafford.com

Most Trafford titles are also available at major online book retailers.

Co-authored by Rita Ginsberg.
Edited by Pamela Guerrieri.

© Copyright 2008 Rita Ginsberg.

All rights reserved. No part of this publication may be reproduced, stored in a retrieval system, or transmitted, in any form or by any means, electronic, mechanical, photocopying, recording, or otherwise, without the written prior permission of the author.

Note for Librarians: A cataloguing record for this book is available from Library and Archives Canada at www.collectionscanada.ca/amicus/index-e.html

ISBN: 978-1-4251-8653-1

We at Trafford believe that it is the responsibility of us all, as both individuals and corporations, to make choices that are environmentally and socially sound. You, in turn, are supporting this responsible conduct each time you purchase a Trafford book, or make use of our publishing services. To find out how you are helping, please visit www.trafford.com/responsiblepublishing.html

Our mission is to efficiently provide the world's finest, most comprehensive book publishing service, enabling every author to experience success. To find out how to publish your book, your way, and have it available worldwide, visit us online at www.trafford.com/10510

www.trafford.com

North America & international
toll-free: 1 888 232 4444 (USA & Canada)
phone: 250 383 6864 ♦ fax: 250 383 6804
email: info@trafford.com

The United Kingdom & Europe
phone: +44 (0)1865 487 395 ♦ local rate: 0845 230 9601
facsimile: +44 (0)1865 481 507 ♦ email: info.uk@trafford.com

10 9 8 7 6 5 4 3 2 1

Dedicated to the Memory of

FRED GREHL

(January 7, 1924 – February 16, 2006)

Author's Acknowledgements

I am deeply grateful to my children, who believed my life was a story worth telling, and the hours and effort my daughter Rita Ginsberg dedicated to the completion of this manuscript. I am thankful for the encouragement and patience my family has shown me, and I give special thanks to my granddaughter, Heather McCaskill, for her suggestions and edits as we drafted the first manuscript for this book.

I would like to thank Pamela Guerrieri the Senior Editor and Project Coordinator at Proofed to Perfection for her diligent review who helped me frame my story proudly to pass on to future generations of readers. She is a talented copyeditor and accommodating person we came to know through the Trafford Talent Pool.

Leni Schick-Grehl

Contents

PREFACE IX

MY PARENTS AND FAMILY LIFE 1

MY BIRTH AND CHILDHOOD 6

MY FATHER'S MOTORCYCLE 11

MY SCHOOL YEARS 15

SUMMER VACATIONS 20

CHRISTMAS TRADITIONS 27

HITLER'S RISE TO POWER 31

THE BEAUTY SALON 34

MARDI GRAS 1939 42

INVASION OF POLAND 46

MY BOYFRIEND 48

TRIP TO ZELL VINEYARDS 58

AIR RAIDS OF 1944 62

GERMANY SURRENDERED 72

JOURNEY TO BREMEN 75

I REACH OMA'S HOUSE 81

THE AMERICAN SOLDIER 86

A NIGHT AT THE USO DANCE 90

THE ENGAGEMENT PARTY	97
FRED GOES HOME	99
AFTER THE WAR	101
FRED'S LETTER	104
I LEAVE FOR AMERICA	107
OUR WEDDING DAY	118
OUR FIRST HOUSE	121
MY FATHER'S NEW BUSINESS	124
STARTING A FAMILY	127
THE AMERICAN DREAM	134

Preface

My story is not something you can pick up on a bookshelf. Volumes of books have been written about the calamities of war, the holocaust, and the campaigns and strategies that changed history. But our lives were deeper than that. There was joy, love, and hope for humanity.

This book was written for my children, grandchildren, great-grandchildren, and for generations to come who ask; "What was it like to grow up in Nazi Germany?" It presents the accounts of my parent's lives in Germany before I was born, my hometown, schooling, and growing up along the backdrop of World War II.

It was my children who inspired me to tell my story, a legacy of love, friendship, and new beginnings to remind the world to embrace life and learn from the mistakes of generations past.

> "What lies behind us
> and what lies before us
> are tiny matters
> compared to what lies within us."
> **Oliver W. Holmes**

Deutschland

x

CHAPTER 1

My Parents and Family Life

My mother, Johanne Göhner, called "Hanni" for short, was born to Helene and August Göhner on June 30, 1898. She grew up in Bremen-Aumund near the Weser River, which enters the North Sea at Bremerhaven in northwest Germany. She was raised alongside five siblings: two sisters and three brothers by the names of Martha, Elli, Emil, August, and Karl.

She met my father, Johann Schick, in 1918 after WWI. It was a period of economic struggle and decline in the value of the German mark during the Depression. He was living in Bremen after the war and they met at a soccer game. Following a year of courtship, they married on November 1, 1919, in Bremen-Aumund, Germany when she was twenty-one years old.

My father's family came from the hazy city of Duisburg; a large industrial area of steel mills, blast furnaces, and coal mines along the Rhine River in the central west region of Germany, near the border of the Netherlands. His parents were Johann and Lambertina Schick, and he was the third eldest child of six siblings, with two brothers and three sisters: Joseph (Yup), Bernhard, Christine, Maria, and Greta.

I'll never forget the day my parents told me the story of how they met in Bremen. I was curled up next to my father on our living room sofa as he recounted the details for me.

Soccer was a very popular sport in Germany and my father, Johann, played on a soccer team when he met my mother, Hanni. While they dated, Hanni attended his games regularly with her friends, boasting how athletic and coordinated he was maneuvering the soccer ball with precision on the field. After they became officially engaged, a friend from Johann's soccer team made a startling remark to him.

"Johann, are you certain you want to marry a woman with a crippled arm?"

"What?" Johann said. "There's nothing wrong with Hanni's arm," he insisted, speaking in her defense.

"I went to school with her and she couldn't use her right arm after an operation she had," he recalled.

Following their discussion, Johann observed how Hanni used her right arm and did not detect any abnormality. Finally, he mustered the courage to ask her about it.

"My friends told me that your right arm is crippled, but I've been watching your arm and it looks normal to me," he said. "Is there something wrong with it?"

"No, my right arm is fine, but you have been watching the wrong arm!" she laughed. "I had an operation on my left arm when I was a young girl," she revealed.

Hanni explained that when she was twelve years old her arm was bitten by an insect, became severely infected, and refused to heal. Poison from the bite spread into her bone and her doctor wanted to amputate her arm above her elbow. Her mother refused to let him amputate it and begged him to try and save her arm. The doctor brought in a specialist who decided to attempt an operation that would remove the infected tissue and bone surrounding her elbow. The surgery proved successful, but she suffered great pain, scars, and permanent immobility of her arm at the elbow. After months of physical therapy, she regained limited use of her arm and fingers, but she learned to adapt, and she concealed it well. Her arm and hand always remained small and dainty, but they never interfered with her daily tasks.

Though Hanni could not straighten out her left arm, Johann had never noticed the defect because she concealed it by always holding her purse. She never talked about her arm and wore long sleeves to hide it. All along he had thought she looked like the Queen of England, clutching her purse close to her chest—dignified and confident as she strolled. He loved her all the more for it.

Johann asked for Hanni's hand in marriage and they had an intimate wedding with family and friends in Aumund. The wedding reception was held at Hanni's parents', Helene and August Göhner's, home, where Hanni and Johann lived temporarily.

The family, along with Johann's friends, subjected the newlyweds to several practical jokes on their wedding night—a common wedding tradition in their generation. Late in the evening, the newlyweds slipped upstairs to their private quarters. Upon shutting the bedroom door, the guests rushed outside and circled the house clanging pots and pans like noisemakers to poke fun at them! But that was only the beginning. When Johann and Hanni climbed onto the bed, it collapsed, plunging them into a tub of water hidden under it! The pranksters had deliberately fractured the support boards so the bed would break, dropping them and their featherbed into the water. Johann flung the bedroom window open and shouted obscenities to the crowd below, but everyone simply burst into laughter and resumed clanging their pots and pans.

Johann and Hanni remained in Aumund for several months after their wedding. Johann worked temporarily with August Göhner, his father-in-law at the Steingut ceramic factory in Bremen-Vegasack making ceramic pottery, flower pots, and fine porcelain figurines, but soon was laid off. After losing his job he moved to Duisburg to find work. His younger brothers, Joseph and Bernhard, and his father worked at the August Thyssen-Huette steel mills in Duisburg-Bruckhausen. Johann found work at the same factory and the newlyweds moved into an apartment near Bruckhausen.

After WWI, the value of the German mark was practically worthless. A loaf of bread could cost a thousand marks due to the economy's hyperinflation. Sometimes families burned their currency notes in their stoves for heat because it would burn longer than the amount of firewood they could buy with it.

French infantry occupied Germany from 1919 to 1930 to secure war reparation payments incurred during the war. During this time, they enforced nightly curfews and behaved wildly, even when on guard duty. It wasn't safe on the streets because of the many intoxicated soldiers, often behaving erratically with their weapons.

Johann's mother, Lambertina, would rush to the corner store after the boys were paid to buy bread and deli meat before the onset of curfew. In addition to the looming curfew, she needed to buy groceries as soon as they got paid because the value of the German mark could decline even more by the next morning. The lesser the value of the mark, the lesser amount of food she could buy.

One afternoon, she was determined to run out to the delicatessen to buy some food even though it was nearly dark.

My parents, Johanne (Hanni) and Johann Schick married in Bremen, Germany November 1, 1919.

"I'm going to look and see if there are any guards on the street tonight," she said as she opened the front door slightly to look if the coast was clear.

Suddenly, a gunshot rang out. Her family watched in horror as she collapsed to the floor. While she was peeking out of the door, she had been shot in the middle of her head and killed instantly by a French guard. Her death, in 1922, devastated the family and my grandfather. Whether it was deliberate or just a stray bullet from a random gun firing remains a mystery.

CHAPTER 2

My Birth and Childhood

My mother gave birth to me on Monday, June 8, 1924 on the German holiday of Pfingsten (Pentecost Monday) seven weeks after Easter. I recall my mother's story of my birth and her description of the beautiful, summer weather on the day before I was born. It was a Sunday, and distant church bells echoed throughout the city as she opened her apartment windows for some fresh air. She could see the park from her living room window and families were gathering to enjoy an afternoon picnic, dressed in their finest Sunday attire and stylish hats of the 20's era. It seemed like the perfect summer day that could go on forever.

But as the afternoon hours came upon the town, suddenly the sky darkened and a storm rapidly blew in without warning. The park goers quickly gathered their picnic baskets and blankets as the thunder and rain showers forced them from the grassy knoll. My mother was finding it humorous to watch them run for safety in their soaked clothes and wet hair when she suddenly experienced her first labor pain.

She endured the pain of labor into the night. At some point the midwife arrived in her wet and drenched clothing to help deliver me. My mother gave birth to me shortly after midnight to the background of thunderstorms and pounding rain.

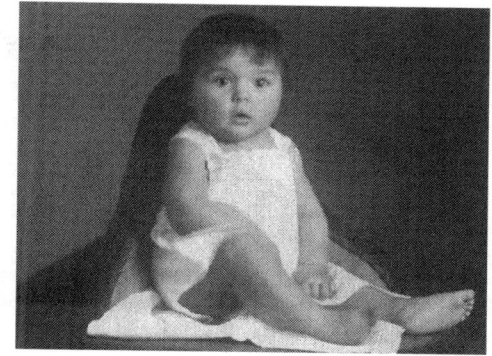

This is a photo of me at six months old.

As my mother heard my first wailing cries at birth, she chuckled and said, "Du kleiner donner schlag!" (You little thunder bolt!) She continued to call me her little thunder bolt in childhood whenever she became flustered with me.

I was named after my grandmother (oma), Helene Göhner, but called Leni, my baptism name, growing up. We lived in Marlox, a small district of Duisburg throughout my childhood at Hagedornstraße 25. I remained my parents' only child—cheerful, curious, and bright for my age.

I clearly remember my obsession with my hair—combing and fixing it continuously—beginning around the age of three. My mother regularly took me to the beauty shop to have my hair cut professionally and I always kept it neatly combed.

My Uncle August, an amateur photographer, came over to take our pictures. Once outside he directed me where to stand.

"Leni, stand over here by the flowers to have your picture taken," he said. But, instead of posing for him as he asked, I said, "Mus mich cammen," (I must comb) and I scampered off into the house. My parents laughed at my childish antics and waited for me to return from combing my hair. However, when I came back my mother was astounded when she looked at me.

I was three years old when my mother's brother, Uncle August took a picture of me after I cut my hair.

"Oh no! What have you done to your hair?" she exclaimed, realizing that I had cut my hair and bangs when I went into the house.

"I fixed it," I cried.

"You cut your hair off!" she said as she shook her finger at me with a vengeance. However, despite her disapproval of my haircut, my Uncle August snapped a picture of me with my long face and remarked, "Oh Hanni, she just wants to be a hairdresser someday."

In addition to my preoccupation with my own hair, I styled my dolls hair with beautiful ringlets and curls I made by brushing sections of their hair around my finger. They had real human hair that I meticulously maintained.

Although I did not have a lot of dolls growing up, one Christmas I received an exquisite, top of the line German doll that stood about two feet tall, with beautiful features, glass eyes, and real brown hair. She had rubber hands with jointed arms and legs for posing her body. She even walked and talked. When I maneuvered her arms up and down, she walked while moving her head from side to side saying, "Mama." She became my favorite doll along with a boy doll I called Karlheinz. I proudly paraded them around in their many outfits nestled in the elaborate doll carriage that my father bought at the doll makers shop.

I played well with my imagination and entertained myself since I didn't have playmates most of the time. My father used his carpentry skills to build me a play store that I could stand behind and pretend to sell real food to my dolls. The unique storefront included a counter tailored to my height, with drawers and cupboards to store food, including a bin for sugar and flour. I had a small scale to weigh my food and a register with coins in it. It had sliding glass doors that I would open when a customer arrived. My dolls each had their own basket to carry their food in and my father made each one a stand to prop them up in front of my store.

My mother bought me brussels sprouts that I sold as cabbage, baby carrots and small potatoes for my store. My mother also bought me marzipan candy that cake decorators used to mold into shapes and animals. I had colored marzipan that looked like a loaf of bread and realistic looking chickens and pigs that I pretended to sell at my counter. Every now and then, my mother would buy a chicken from me so she could eat the marzipan.

We did not have refrigeration, so meat was bought daily at the butcher shop and bread from the local bakery. The butcher would wrap the meat she bought in paper and place it into Mother's basket. She would buy fresh vegetables and eggs at the town market and the merchants would take a sheet of paper and twist it into a large cone and put the items she bought into it, because stores did not have grocery bags. Then she would fold it closed and tuck it in her tote bag or basket to take home. My mother made me tiny paper cones to put my produce and vegetables into when I made a sale to my dolls.

My mother was a wonderful seamstress, and I had beautiful clothes. She taught me how to sew by hand and I made some clothes for my dolls. Whenever my parents would take me with them to their friends' houses, I would usually sit by myself in the corner and sew or crochet doll clothes to occupy myself while they were socializing. I learned to depend on myself for my own entertainment.

I got my first bicycle at four years old. On a frosty morning my father took me on my first bike ride. The bike lacked any brakes and the pedals kept spinning around until I put my feet on the ground to stop. It didn't take me long to learn to peddle and I did a good job keeping up with my father as we went for a ride in front of our house.

His bicycle had a headlight mounted to it since he often came home in the dark. It worked without batteries or kerosene. He poured carbide powder into one chamber and water into the top chamber. When the water dripped onto the powder it produced a gas that he could ignite. He could adjust the size of the flame so that the light reflected more brightly inside the headlamp to improve his visibility in the dark.

My mother's bicycle had a basket on it and she would bring my father his lunch each day to work. She also brought me my lunch when I started school. Most people rode bicycles to work, or commuted by streetcars. Merchants still made deliveries by horse-drawn wagons or carts down the narrow cobblestone streets and alleyways in the city. Automobiles were a rare luxury of the wealthy; however, motorcycles were growing in popularity and a prestigious commodity my father longed for.

CHAPTER 3

My Father's Motorcycle

My father and mother saved their money to buy a motorcycle for travel. Though just five years old, I still remember the day he came home with a black Horex 500 motorcycle with a sidecar passenger seat for me. His face gleamed with excitement as he kick-started the engine and revved it up with a twist of his wrist on the handlebars. "Do you want to go for a ride in the sidecar?" he asked me with enthusiasm. He sat me in the sidecar and I squealed with excitement as he accelerated down our street. His new motorcycle, and the opportunity to travel as a family around the country, filled him with pride. My parents enjoyed the freedom of traveling the countryside of the Rhineland and to destinations in the Netherlands that were not feasible by train or streetcar.

Our travels to Holland were especially pleasant in the springtime, marked by passing fields of colorful tulips and Dutch windmills decorating the countryside. The centuries old cities of Amsterdam and Rötterdam boasted narrow streets, cafes, monuments, and old churches to see. Amsterdam, famous for its small boat canals throughout the city, resembled a romantic version of Venice.

I rode in the sidecar while my mother sat behind my father during our scenic trips and excursions to Holland in the early

1930's. Holland bordered Germany to the northwest and my mother loved to travel there to buy coffee.

"The flavor and aroma of the coffee from Holland is so much better than the coffee we buy here in Germany," she said.

However, a duty charge applied to any items they declared as they passed through customs. My mother hid her coffee beans to avoid the tax by pouring the beans into a nylon stocking and wrapping it around her waist, then securing her corset over the beans to conceal it. She never declared her beans and never got caught.

Whenever their coffee was getting low my father suggested that we take a trip into Holland to buy some, just for the opportunity for an outing on his motorcycle. He loved riding and dressed up in his retro brown leather jacket, pants and high riser laced boots. Women did not wear pants in the 30's, so my mother sewed herself skirt pants that gave her the freedom to straddle the seat of the motorcycle without worry of her skirt flying up in the wind. I rode in the sidecar wherever they went. It was an exhilarating experience, especially when my father took a sharp curve too quickly and I hung on for dear life, for fear of being tossed out into the countryside somewhere.

Often, my parents would take motorcycle outings with other couples. It became a popular pastime with them, attending regular excursions together as a motorcycle club. They rode through surrounding villages and communities on Sunday afternoons, often heading to Düsseldorf (south of Duisburg) to the sidewalk cafes for an afternoon coffee and dessert. As I got older, I thought it was too boring to go with them and their friends. Sometimes they would stop in the country and hang hammocks in the trees and nap for a while, leaving me with nothing to do. Once, I asked their friends to play hide-and-seek with me. They

My parent's on their Horex motorcycle. It was a well known German motorcycle brand of the "Horex – Fahrzeugbau AG", founded in 1923 in Bad Hamburg by Fritz Kleemann.

said, "Sure, you go hide and we will find you." I hid for a long time and no one came looking for me. When I finally came out, they were sleeping in their hammocks! Eventually, my parents let me stay with Aunt Maria, my father's sister with nine children. I had more fun staying with them than being around adults most of the time.

Occasionally my Aunt Maria came over in the afternoon to enjoy Mother's great coffee and dessert she bought in Holland. Aunt Maria had her oldest child of nine baby-sit the younger children when she visited my mother. It was her only opportunity to gossip with Hanni over a cup of coffee.

My father (left), my mother, and friends standing in front of the Köln Cathedral in 1932 while on a motorcycle outing.

CHAPTER 4

My School Years

In 1930, at the age of six, I started first grade at a Catholic school two blocks from where we lived. On my first day of school I toted a new chalkboard and abacus for math to class in a brown shoulder bag my mother bought for my school supplies. I found my way to my first grade classroom and teacher, Fraulein Wren, who would teach me through the sixth grade.

She assigned seats to the thirty-five children, with the boys on one side of the room and the girls on the other. I proudly had an aisle seat. Once we were seated, she grasped her black stick and slapped it formidably against her desk to get everyone's attention. "There will be no talking amongst you in my classroom!" she said abruptly. From that moment on, I feared my new teacher, and her black stick.

The same building held elementary through high school classes, and Fraulein Wren taught all of our subjects. I used my chalkboard to practice the alphabet and print numbers. For math, I used my abacus to learn the basics of addition and subtraction. We used flash cards to memorize our math tables and to prepare us for quizzes in class. Sometimes after school we bought penny candy for a treat. I bought some liquorish candy in flat pieces that had math tables imprinted in them like flash cards. While playing outside, I would try to memorize the answers and if I remembered correctly, I would take a lick of my liquorish candy.

We went to school from 8:00 a.m. to 4:30 p.m., Monday through Friday, and a half day on Saturday. Based on Germany's heavy academic school schedule, students completed their high school education by the eighth grade. Following graduation, a student could attend trade school with an apprenticeship program, or go to college.

Before school began, I walked to church to attend early morning catechism at 7:00 a.m. everyday. The priest taught class and we studied Latin. Following our lessons, we all walked to school together.

We had recess around ten o'clock in the morning. My mother came to the school every morning to see me and give me something to eat. I did not have breakfast before catechism in the morning and I had to wait until my mother arrived.

She rode her bicycle to the school and waited behind the fence with other young mothers for us to come out for a short recess. Usually, I came running down the steps of the school, anxiously looking for my mother, always excited to see her waiting at the edge of the schoolyard wall.

"What did you bring me?" I asked, as I peered curiously over the brick wall to catch a peak of something good. She would reach over the wall through the iron bars to hand me my snack. Sometimes my mother made me a "brötchen" (hot roll) or bread with a boiled egg and hot chocolate. She came back at lunchtime to drop off dinner for me and then she scurried off to take my father his dinner at work. She made him hot meals that she put inside a covered enameled container with compartments to keep the food separated. I remember her home cooking, often making sauerbraten (pot roast marinated in vinegar and seasoning), rolraden (thinly sliced round steak, rolled with onions inside), potato dumplings, potato pancakes with applesauce, and even pig knuckles and sauerkraut. She wrapped the container with towels to help keep the food warm and placed it in the basket on her bicycle. Preparing our meals and delivering them to us each day kept her busy, regardless of the weather.

My childhood memories of Fraulein Wren contrasted sharply with the fond memories of my mother. Fraulein Wren—a miserable person and callous teacher—made most students fear her. She would walk up and down the aisle while we worked on our lessons and whack the table or our hands with a stick if we looked like we had fallen into a daydream. Church and schools had the authority to discipline children without the consent of the parents. Harsh discipline was common and my mother warned me to behave. "Do your lessons and listen to your teacher," she said.

On one occasion, the girl sitting next to me was talking to a classmate. Fraulein Wren, furious, reached for her but couldn't grab her. She snatched me instead and pulled me out of my seat by my earlobe, cutting my ear from the earring I was wearing. Then she made everyone lineup in the front of the classroom to await punishment. She used her stick to switch the boys on their butts and the girls on the palms of our hands. The swish of her stick delivered a painful blow that left a burning welt in my hands. I tearfully returned to my seat after the ordeal. Fraulein Wren punished the entire class, regardless of who misbehaved.

When I went home my mother noticed some blood on my dress. "What is this on your dress?" she asked curiously.

"Fraulein Wren pulled my ear today and hit my hands when I didn't do anything wrong," I cried.

She listened carefully to me while she cleaned my sore ear, and then remarked, "Your ear will be fine tomorrow along with your broken pride." And, then she gave me a hug to ease my pain and humiliation.

Throughout my early years of schooling, Fraulein Wren was disliked by the students and their parents. On one occasion someone took revenge on her. During class there was a knock on the door and Fraulein Wren went to the door and opened it. We all turned our heads to see who was there, but instead all we saw was a black umbrella strike her over her head as she fell to the floor, passing out. The culprit disappeared quickly and I don't think she ever found out who it was.

Fortunately, I got a new teacher in sixth through eighth grade named Fraulein Winter. She was the nicest nun and loved by all of the students. When we completed a subject she allowed us to stand up, stretch, and even exercise with some jumping jacks or stretching exercises, like touching our toes, before we started the next subject. In the middle of the day she would sing a song with us to break up the monotony.

In early elementary school we learned German handwriting in a style called Suetterlin script taught from 1915 to 1941. During our handwriting lessons we practiced the alphabet while singing a limerick in German to make the strokes and sharp angles of the letters more accurately. "Auf und runter und ein punchen drauf." (Up and down and a punctuation dot.) The limerick is lost in the English translation, but useful in German to help develop our writing skills.

Most Bibles, books, and documents were printed in an ornate Fraktur type style we diligently studied in art class. We created ornate letters on paper using a calligraphy pen with exchangeable tips that we dipped into an ink well before each pen stoke. We drew each letter of the alphabet first, and then we would embellish each letter with flowers, curvy swirls, and strokes to create a beautiful piece of artwork using our imagination.

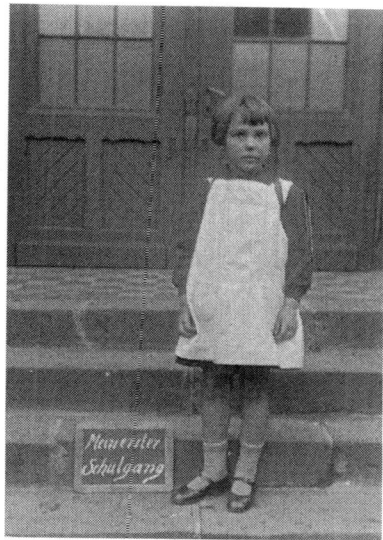

Me on my first day of school, posing by a sign that reads: "Mein erster schulgang" (My first school day) in 1930.

The Catholic school I attended on Henriettenstraß first through eighth grade.

A photo with my parents when I started school in 1930.

CHAPTER 5

Summer Vacations

Each summer I had six weeks of school vacation. I spent many summers at my grandparents' house in Aumund. My mother wrote Oma (Grandma) a letter to let her know when I would arrive and she would pick me up. At just six years old I started taking the train on my own. She bought me train tickets for a locked cabin that I sat in during the trip to Bremen. I wore the tickets on a string around my neck and the conductor would let me out when we reached my destination and escorted me off of the train to meet my oma. The train was always on schedule, but very slow, stopping at each town before it arrived in Bremen. I left around 10:00 a.m. and arrived around 5:00 p.m. in the afternoon.

Oma sat anxiously waiting for me at the train station, waving as the train made its final approach. I could barely contain my excitement and looked forward to spending the summer with her. I was her only granddaughter and she lavished me with attention and spoiled me with new school clothes. She rode her bicycle from Aumund to Vegasack, another district of Bremen on the Weser River. Then she boarded a ferry boat with her bicycle to ride up the river to Bremen to pick me up at the train station. We took the ferry back to Vegasack and then walked the rest of the way home with my suitcase in her bicycle basket.

By the time we got home, hunger had crept in and she made me a sandwich on the bread plate she kept just for me. I had my own bedroom to sleep in since her children were grown up and married. Her son Emil lived next door with his son Karlheinz, who was a couple of years younger than me. He was the only cousin I had to play with when I visited my grandparents.

My Aunt Marta, my mother's oldest sister, lived around the corner but she never had children. Karlheinz and I had fun together hiking through the wheat field across the street and climbing Oma's fruit trees. Apple, pear, and plum trees grew by the side of her house and she made jelly preserves, canned fruit, and vegetables for the winter.

She also had a vegetable garden where I learned how to pull up potatoes, pick beans, carrots and weed the garden with a hoe. If I wasn't helping her in the garden, I was learning to sew. Oma sewed clothes by making her own patterns and she taught me how to make patterns for my dolls. She would buy enough material to make a dress for me and my doll. By the time I returned to school she had created a new wardrobe for me. My Aunt Marta came over and taught me to embroider, crotchet and knit for my dolls. I occupied much of my time on vacation making doll clothes with her. She had a cheerful outlook on life although she was often absentminded and distracted with other things. But, from her I learned that anything wrong can be made right, if you used a little bit of ingenuity! It is inevitable to make some mistakes when learning needlework, and whenever Marta came over to Oma's to sew with us, she would make a mistake that Oma would catch. "Marta, this doesn't look right," she said in a tone of puzzlement.

"Oh Momma," she called Oma. "I'll just make a blümchin (flower) over it," and she did just that. What was amazing is that it looked more beautiful after she covered her mistake.

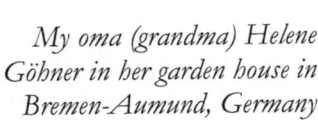
My oma (grandma) Helene Göhner in her garden house in Bremen-Aumund, Germany

While the women gathered to sew in the afternoons, my opa (grandpa) attended to his animals and chores. He raised a pig each year in a pen behind the house. He also grew wheat in a plot of land he owned across the street from their house. He piled his wagon up with the wheat he cut and I rode in it while he pulled me to the mill in Vegasack. There, he would have the wheat ground into the grain that he used as filler in the pigs' food and feed for his chickens and carrier pigeons. Once the pigs were big and fat, he slaughtered them and smoked the meat in the smokehouse behind the house.

His carrier pigeons were raised in a shed behind the house as well and I watched him band their legs to identify them. He trained them to fly long distances back to their roost, timed them, and sold them for profit. Carrier pigeons delivered messages to the front lines in WWI when radio communication was not available or reliable. After the war, people enjoyed racing their pigeons in competitions.

My opa was a hard-working man but enjoyed an occasional drink of Schnapps on a Sunday morning while Oma prepared the dinner meal. Sunday was Opa's day of rest and relaxation with his friends and neighbors. Some mornings he sat on his bench outside next to the lilac bushes; overgrown and draped in fragrant blossoms in the summertime. He shared his flask of schnapps with his neighbor and asked me to get him some more.

"Leni, take these coins to Willtack (a tavern around the corner) and ask the bartender to fill my flask with some schnapps that has a little speck (yellow tint, not clear) to it."

"Yes, Opa," I answered, and I scampered off to the tavern to get it for him. It was acceptable in those days to do that, without questions asked.

Sometimes, Opa would go to Vegasack to the Grauer Esel (Gray Donkey) tavern on Sunday morning, dressed in his suit, tie, dress hat, and walking stick, looking very distinguished and proper for a Sunday gathering with his friends. Oma would send me along with him, most likely to ensure that he got home in time for dinner. The men usually took turns buying a round of beer or drinks in the tavern, while I had a soft drink. A few times Opa had too much to drink when the men insisted on buying another round and he stumbled into the ditch along the road coming home. But, I helped him up and we always made it home in time for dinner.

My oma busied herself in the kitchen on Sunday mornings preparing dinner and dessert for their afternoon kaffee klatsch (afternoon coffee and desert). One of her favorite desserts was a plum fruit kuchen coffee cake baked with her plums, sliced and layered on top, with a glaze sauce poured over the fruit. She would prepare the batter and fruit on a large baker's pan that didn't fit in her small oven, so she took it to the corner bakery in the morning to ask them to bake it for her and she would pick it up in the afternoon. The bakery offered this service to the neighborhood homemakers as a common courtesy. Sometimes, Uncle Emil and Karlheinz joined us for dessert. Dinner was our warm meal of the day in the early afternoon, and cold cuts and bread was primarily served for our evening meal.

My oma made me eggs for breakfast sometimes, but one day she was in a joking mood and took a couple of eggs from the carrier pigeon's nest and cooked them for me.

"Leni, I made something special for you this morning," she said.

I sat down and she served me the tiniest eggs I ever saw! They were cooked sunny side up, sitting in the middle of my giant plate.

"Little eggs for little girls," she said with a smile. And, I giggled and laughed while I ate them.

Following breakfast, my Aunt Marta came over and asked Oma if she could take me to the beach along the Weser River. It was a hot summer day, perfect for a dip into the river's edge. The Weser River was wide with strong changing currents, fluctuating during low and high tides. Many people were enjoying the beachfront with a lifeguard stationed high on a wooden platform overlooking the beach. Aunt Marta watched me leisurely from her chair in the grass as I sat on the edge of the water, small waves splashing over me. She instructed me to sit at the edge and not venture into the water since I couldn't swim.

Sometimes the waves climbed higher from the ships passing by and they toppled over my head, much to my enjoyment. But this day the tide changed for real and a high wave suddenly scooped me up and pulled me under the water on my way out to sea. Though just six years old at the time, I instinctively grabbed onto the weeds near the shore and did not let go of them when the current pulled against me. To my good fortune, a lifeguard saved me in time and my distraught Aunt Marta never took me to the river again to swim. I missed the river, but there were always many other activities to keep me busy.

Oma loved to shop and show me the sights in Bremen and Bremerhaven. We would leave in the morning with our bicycles while my opa (grandpa) worked. I had my own bicycle they bought for me to use during my summer vacations.

We rode our bicycles to Vegasack and boarded a ferry to Bremen. We shopped at the Marktplatz (Market Square) where the statue of Roland stands in the vicinity of the Town Hall and St. Peter's Cathedral (13th century). The statue of Roland (1404) signified the city's protector bearing the "sword of justice" and shield. We also visited the city's oldest section, the Schnoor district; it had narrow cobblestone lanes lined with shops and houses dating back to the 16th century.

My oma took me by train to Bremerhaven to see the ships and sailboats in the harbors. The Weser River enters the North Sea at Bremerhaven and is one of the largest seaports in the world. We saw a sailboat regatta race on the North Sea one afternoon, and ocean liners heading to America. We waved at the people boarding the ships, pretending that we knew them. Oma obtained permission to see what a passenger ship looked like on the inside. Beautiful chandeliers hung in the dining halls and luxurious cabins lined the ship for the passengers. Fascinated by what I saw, I wondered what it would be like to sail the sea. Then, a loud bell rang and they announced that all visitors had to leave the ship. Afterwards, we headed to the market place on our bicycles before our journey back home.

One summer my oma took me to Helgoland Island on a large ship so I could experience a cruise on the North Sea. The island, located 70 km (44 miles) from the German coastline, was a popular tourist attraction consisting of two islands. She loved the sea and enjoyed taking me with her for companionship.

The North Sea was very rough, but we never got seasick. We arrived at the island and could see right away why it was famous for its tall rock columns, called Lange Anna (Tall Anna), and beautiful beaches. The ship cruised around the islands and then docked for a few hours to let the passengers stroll along the beaches and visit the famous landmarks before returning to Bremerhaven.

By summer's end I was anxious to return home to my parents and tell them about my adventures. I loved my summer vacations with Oma, and I looked forward to every summer with her.

CHAPTER 6

Christmas Traditions

December 6th marked the beginning of the Christmas season. Fearful whispers passed between young onlookers when St. Nicholas arrived at the community park in his red and white bishop robe, noble hat, and staff. His long snow-white beard dangled from his round chin, and he sat comfortably in a chair with a book on his lap that listed the misdeeds of all the children. By his side stood his sinister companion, Ruprecht. Dressed in a black cape with chains binding his ankles, Ruprecht's face hid beneath a layer of black soot. In one hand he carried a sack of coal, and in the other a rod for disobedient children.

As each child approached St. Nicholas, his eyes searched through his big book to see who was naughty and who was nice. Each child would recite a poem or sing a song to make their plea that they were good children. If St. Nicholas was pleased, he would smile and give them a piece of candy. Otherwise, Ruprecht gave them a piece of coal and a switch on their behind.

When it was my turn to walk up the steps and face him, I trembled as I stood in front of him. With a clenched jaw he flipped the pages of his book while I stared timidly up at him. As he muttered, "Um-hmm," pointing to a page in his book, I began to recite the poem that my mother taught me:

"Lieber gutter Weinachsman schau mich nicht so böse an, ich will doch immer artich sein." (Dear good Christmas man, please don't look at me so mean, for I will be good from now on.) He smiled at me, handed me a piece of candy and sent me on my way.

In the following years, when I was seven or eight years old, I began to question if St. Nicholas was in fact real. The next time I stepped up to him I yanked his beard, but it didn't come off! I thought to myself, "He's the real one!" I was so startled that I don't remember if I was switched by Ruprecht or not, but I didn't doubt his authenticity again.

Every Christmas Eve began around six o'clock in the evening at our home. My mother would remind me the morn of Christmas Eve, "You cannot be in this room when the Christ Child comes, but we must help prepare for his coming. Please stay in your room while we get the tree ready." I would wait impatiently in my room, sometimes passing the minutes by sitting on the steps leading to the hallway. When the clock struck six o'clock, I would walk down to the end of the hallway and wait for them to call me in. Excitement rushed through me in anticipation of their invitation, for I would not see the decorated tree or presents until my parents opened up the door to the living room for me to enter.

When the door finally opened, a radiant Christmas tree lit the room with twinkling sparklers to represent the spirit of the Christ Child leaving gifts, and brightly lit candles glistened on the tree. It was carefully decorated with glass bulbs, tinsel, and bird ornaments clipped to the tree branches with the candles held firmly in place by reflective tin trays to capture the wax drippings. The unwrapped presents were arranged carefully under the tree for me to see everything. Brilliantly decorated plates called "teller foll" were left for each of us, loaded with nuts, apples, oranges, chocolate, and marzipan. Plates of spritz cookies and stollen bread (a moist heavy loaf of braided bread filled with raisins and dried fruit) decorated my mother's table and remained a family tradition each year.

As I played with my new toys, my father tuned his radio to a station broadcasting the "Bells of Christmas." We listened for an hour to the cathedral church bells chiming across Germany while he sat comfortably in his chair with a glass of fresh eggnog, a smile, and a handful of spritz cookies.

Christmas Day invited the scents of our upcoming feast throughout our home. A banquet of plump roast goose and stuffing awaited us, followed by a traditional lighting of the Christmas tree. Several weeks before Christmas they purchased a goose they kept in a cage to fatten up for Christmas dinner. Once the bird was killed, my mother pulled and saved all of its feathers to stuff her pillows with. After dinner we visited Aunt Maria and Uncle Franz with their nine children. Each child received a decorated plate of nuts, fruit, and marzipan. Uncle Franz was a magnificent carver, creating a nativity scene by hand with intricate details.

When I entered my teenage years, my mother wanted to do something special for me on Christmas. She ordered a specially made dress in royal blue velvet and pink satin that I dearly loved. The sleeves were tailored with pleats in the pink satin around the wrist and puffed velvet sleeves around the elbows fashioned for a young lady my age.

In addition, she wanted to find me a gift basket filled with girlish toiletries, creams and designer perfume she loved called 4711 Eau de Cologne. She came upon a beautiful basket designed as a birdcage at a chocolate store. She purchased it along with a colorful foil wrapped chocolate parakeet to string up inside the cage. Unfortunately, the string broke while she was tying it up and the chocolate broke into pieces. She decided to go back to the store and get another one. As she was walking home on Christmas Eve it was sleeting outside and she slipped and fell, breaking the second parakeet. She went back the third time to the store and bought another parakeet, praying that this one wouldn't break. She finished tying it up in time to put it under the tree for Christmas Eve. To my delight, it was one of the loveliest gifts I ever received as a teenager. By my expression of appreciation, my mother knew it was worth the effort and calamity she experienced to make it for me.

CHAPTER 7

Hitler's Rise to Power

In 1931, while Germany was in a state of economic depression, Adolph Hitler traveled around the country making political speeches. He promised to restore the economy and create new jobs for the masses in an effort to gain prestige and votes for the Nazi Party.

By 1932, the Nazi Party was gaining strength in popularity through its mass distribution of literature and propaganda, building racist and anti-Semitism against the Jews. It wasn't apparent from the beginning what a monster he really was. But as time went on, the Nazi Party began to intimidate with terror to ensure loyalty and Hitler's victory to rule as Chancellor of Germany.

My father became a victim of their violence when walking home one afternoon in 1932. Propaganda flyers were handed out at every street corner he passed. His pockets were so stuffed with them that he tossed away the next flyer handed to him. The officer shouted obscenities and accusations at him and began beating him in the street. Only two weeks earlier he had a stomach operation and he tried to protect his stomach the best he could by pulling his knees up into a fetal position. Other members of the Nazi Party joined in the violence and kicked him, brutally breaking his ribs and bones. A passing bicyclist jumped off his bike and began beating my father on his head and face with his bicycle pump, knocking out all of his teeth and breaking his nose. They left him lying on the street in agony. I don't know how he got home.

At only eight years I witnessed Hitler's wrath when I came home from school and saw what they did to my father. He survived the beatings and concealed his animosity to protect us.

I remember that he got false teeth after he recovered from his attack, with a gold tooth made from his wedding band to look like a gold filling.

Hitler became Chancellor of Germany in 1933, marking the beginning of his dictatorship and the genocide of the Jewish communities.

My grandfather, August Göhner's youngest brother Bernhard, lived in Bremen, Germany. Between 1935 and 1938 my Great Uncle Bernhard would travel to Duisburg by train to visit my father. One time I overheard him tell my father that he helped some people sneak several Jews into Holland. My father got involved in these endeavors as well, though I'm not clear on the specifics. He frequently drove his motorcycle into Amsterdam and Rötterdam, Holland, before the war began, and gave addresses and maps to Uncle Bernhard. I slowly figured out that they were trying to help the underground somehow, but I never said a word to anyone.

A Jewish family, the Hertz family, lived in my neighborhood and owned a store selling light fixtures and gas lanterns. I played ball and hop scotch with their two children. The brother was one year older than me and his sister was younger and very sweet. They both had blond hair and they didn't look Jewish. One day, I saw them playing on the street after school and I wanted to join them, but the brother said to me, "We can't play with you anymore or you will get into trouble," and they both went home. I didn't understand why and returned home very upset.

Soon afterwards, their store was demolished along with several others. It must have happened during the night; the Nazis destroyed everything. While crossing Wilhem Street, I saw other storefronts shattered, including a dress shop. At first I thought I saw dead bodies laying in the store and on the sidewalk, but they were just manikins. Frightened, I dashed home to tell my mother. Sadly, I never saw the Jewish brother and sister again after that and we never found out what happened to the families.

A friend of mine lived in the apartment next door and I used to style her hair in ringlets. Her father worked for the railroad and was friends with my father. One afternoon we visited them and while playing in the bedroom with my friend I overheard crying in the room where our fathers were. I naturally perked up to hear the conversation. My friend's father told my father that he saw Jewish families crammed onto the boxcars and little children begged him for water. When he fetched a bucket of water to give them an SS officer cocked a rifle to his head and threatened to shoot him if he proceeded. My friend's father, traumatized from the experience, needed to confide in someone, and trusted my father's word to secrecy.

CHAPTER 8

The Beauty Salon

I Graduated high school in the spring of 1938 at the age of thirteen. My mother wanted me to attend trade school after graduation to become a seamstress. She had great expectations for me and even bought me a sewing machine for my apprenticeship program. A wonderful seamstress herself, she was certain that I would follow in her footsteps.

It was about a week before Easter and a friend of my mother's asked me to fix her hair one evening because she didn't have time to go to the salon before Easter Sunday. I happily agreed to the task. While I was combing her hair she candidly said, "I usually have my hair done at Werner Ihnen's beauty salon at 32 Wilhem Street not far from here. Do you know where that is?"

"Yes, I think it's about five blocks from here," I replied.

"He is looking for a girl to start working there and I think that you would enjoy it. Did you ever think about becoming a hairdresser?" she asked.

"Not really. My mother wants me to be a seamstress and she already bought me a sewing machine," I said modestly.

When she left that evening, I started thinking about how much I enjoyed curling and styling hair more than sewing. Perhaps she was right. After giving it some thought I decided that I would much rather be a hairdresser than a dressmaker.

My photo taken when I was fourteen years old following my graduation from high school.

The next day, I went to the salon without my mother's knowledge and asked Mr. Ihnen about the job. The busy, well-kept salon served both men and women. In the front, facing the street, was a barbershop, and in back, a beauty salon with sinks and hair dryers. Mr. Ihnen was in the barbershop with a customer when I walked in and he asked me to have a seat.

Mr. Ihnen stood tall and lean and looked to be in his thirties. He held a comb in his left hand and barber shears in the other, clipping and combing his customer's hair methodically. Once he finished cutting the man's hair he introduced himself as the master barber and proprietor of the salon and asked how he could help me. I introduced myself and asked him if he was looking for a girl to start working as an apprentice at his salon. He said he was and asked my age.

"I am thirteen, but I will be fourteen in June," I said confidently.

He continued asking me more questions and then looked down at my legs inquisitively and said, "Ya, you look like you have strong enough legs for the job. You can start tomorrow, but I will need your parents consent first."

I was thrilled and said, "Yes sir!" and ran home to break the news to my mother.

My mother was stunned with disbelief after all of the arrangements she had already made for me. She asked me over and over again if I was certain that I really wanted to be a hairdresser. To convince her I explained, "If I make a mistake cutting a piece of material, it will be ruined. But, if I make a wrong cut on someone's hair it can grow back!"

"That's true," she said meekly, "We will discuss it with your father when he gets home." Both my parents accepted my decision and gave Mr. Ihnen their consent for me to start. I began working the following morning on Good Friday.

Mr. Ihnen worked in the barbershop with his two younger brothers, Helmut and Kurt. His wife managed the beauty salon and I assisted her and the barbers. A young girl finished her third year as an apprentice and was leaving the salon. Another student replaced her, and I filled the new position as a first year apprentice.

The salon was very busy and I was responsible for sweeping the floors, washing the salon towels on the washboard, hanging them to dry, and cleaning the salon. In the afternoon, I made them lunch of boiled eggs and soup on a gas burner in the back corner of the salon. The shop stayed open very late, with many customers. After they closed, I had to clean and polish the floor. When I finished, Mr. Ihnen said, "Since it is very late you may as well sleep in the barber chair tonight instead of going home." My mother grew worried about me and came to the salon around midnight to see if I was alright.

Mr. Ihnen spoke to my mother; "I'm going to keep her here tonight because I need her to start work by 6:00 o'clock tomorrow morning. She will be fine sleeping in the barber chair tonight," he insisted. Feeling reassured that I was safe she returned home and I fell asleep in the barber chair.

I worked for Mr. Ihnen for one year before my apprenticeship contract could be signed to fulfill my one-year Pfichtjahr of mandatory service to the country, decreed in 1938–1939. He paid me a weekly wage. Once my apprenticeship contract was signed, I earned a weekly rate of two marks the first year, three marks the second year, and five marks the third year. If I would have quit during my apprenticeship program, I would have been fined a large sum of money. However, I continued to work for Mr. Ihnen and saved my money in the bank.

During my apprenticeship, the Nazi organization ordered that all young students attend Hitler's Youth Group meetings and classes each week. My parents could not object to the Fuehrer's laws or orders without risk of terrible punishment or fines by the Nazis. I'm sure that my parents privately conveyed their concerns to my boss and he persuaded the Nazi organization to keep me out. He secretly disagreed with compulsory classes and allegiance of the Nazi Youth Groups; brainwashing recruited children to perform dreadful acts of violence and hatred against family and neighbors for the Nazi Party. Children often reported incriminating information about their parents, not realizing what the consequences could mean for their families.

Mr. Ihnen, a shrewd, persuasive man, convinced the Nazi's that he needed me at work since his brothers and young barbers were drafted into the army. Work was the only qualification for exemption. When they began to hold classes on Sunday mornings for young people who were unable to attend on weekdays, Mr. Ihnen decided to open his salon on Sunday mornings and I worked. Because he convinced the Nazis he needed me to work, I never once had to attend any meetings.

I always obeyed Mr. Ihnen's authority and rules without protest or disrespect at his salon. However, one day after work it snowed a few inches and my friends wanted me to go sledding with them in the park. On our way there we walked past the beauty salon as Mr. Ihnen and his wife were leaving to go to the movies. They heard us talking on the other side of the street and he recognized my laughter.

"Leni! Where are you going?"

"I am going sledding with my friends," I replied.

"You didn't get my permission first!" he responded.

"But, my mother said I could go," I retaliated.

"Are you questioning my authority?" he said sternly.

"No sir," I said.

"Then go home now and come into work an hour early tomorrow morning to load the stove with coal!"

In utter disappointment, I agreed. It got dark early in the winter and as I walked away I ducked into a doorway. When they were out of sight, I dashed quickly to catch up with my friends and went sledding anyway, disobeying his order. However, I still came into the salon the next morning an hour earlier and lit the stove as he instructed me.

My uniforms got dirty from hauling up the coal each day even though I put an apron over myself. My mother usually washed my uniforms by hand with a scrub board in the kitchen sink. Clothes were hung to dry in our attic during cold weather and on the line outside when it was warm. The apartment building had a manual washing machine downstairs and a boiler pot to heat up the water. The laundry soap came in a bar and she shaved off chunks of it and soaked it in hot water to soften it to a jelly-like consistency, creating good suds. We rocked a heavy wooden handle on top of the washing machine back and forth to agitate the clothes, taking turns pushing and pulling for twenty minutes and never stopping a minute short. Then, we used the hand crank on the wringer to squeeze out the water from the clothes after rinsing them. We didn't have bleach to whiten our sheets, so on a sunny summer day my mother laid the sheets out on the thick grass in the sun to dry. Then she would sprinkle water on them again and let them dry. By doing this over and over, the sun eventually bleached out our sheets.

During my first year at the salon I was primarily an assistant to the hairdressers and barbers. I was responsible for opening up the salon each morning around 7:00 a.m. I would add coal to the stove to warm up the salon in the cold winter months. I also, prepared food and started the coffee. We made our own hair spray and setting solution for waving hair, and I would prepare the products each day. We made gel by mixing water with powder and boiling it until it was thick. Once it cooled, I filled the glass jars.

I also helped Mrs. Ihnen heat up the curling irons in a holder fitted over a gas flame used to curl her customers hair. When the curling iron got cool, she would hand it back to me to reheat it and I would pass her a heated one. As I became more experienced, I could judge the right temperature and test them myself before passing it over. I eventually learned how to twirl the curling irons like a professional, which was a process for cooling them down to prevent singeing the hair. We put waves in the hair with the curling iron. We had more control over hair with body.

Women didn't wash their hair often and they would come back just to touch up the waves. Some women wore a bun in their hair, but they wanted the sides of their hair waved before making the bun. We did finger waving most of time. We had plastic combs that we slid into the hair to push a wave up into shape and another comb inserted in the opposite direction to shape the curve of the wave. The hair was stiff and shiny after the finger waves were done.

A hot water tank was mounted to the wall and we lit the gas pilot to heat up the water to wash our customer's hair. We used wooden rollers that had a slot cut into each end of them. Once we rolled a section of hair, we stretched a rubber band over it and snapped it into place to secure the roller. The salon had a couple of electric hair dryers and a permanent wave machine with connecting curling rods that plugged into it to perm a customer's hair.

I was still a young apprentice when a woman came into the salon asking if she could get her hair cut right away since she was in a hurry. All of the hairdressers were busy, so my boss said, "Leni can do it." I was excited to get my first customer. I was doing a good job, but when I trimmed the hair near her ear, I snipped the top of her ear off. It wasn't a deep cut, but it wouldn't stop bleeding. Everyone in the salon tried to help. We tried a thick ointment the barbers used on small razor cuts, but that didn't work either. Eventually, the bleeding stopped, and miraculously she remained calm and forgiving. Ironically, she was my first customer I had at the salon, and years later she was my very last customer before I resigned.

I attended beauty trade school in the evenings three days a week from seven to nine o'clock. I had homework every evening. One of the most challenging assignments was crafting a human

Students working for Werner Ihnen's barber shop for men and women. From the right is Werner Ihnen, his wife, myself, and other young apprentices in 1943.

hair wig and hairpieces. It was a very tedious process of piecing together the fine mesh material used to make a wig onto a mounted headpiece, then sewing them together with strips of ribbon, while shaping it to the head. Once it was pieced together, I used a small hair hook to weave the hair into place; inserting one hair at a time along the part to make it appear natural, and two or three strands around the top and sides. I could use several strands together on the crown and back of the head. The evening lighting was inadequate so my father made a small light box to illuminate the holes in the fine mesh used in the area for the part. When I finished hooking the individual hairs along the part, I had to sew the piece onto my form before completing my wig. All of the hard work paid off because when I graduated from trade school, I received the top grade in my class on the final examination.

CHAPTER 9

Mardi Gras 1939

In 1939, at nearly fifteen years old, my mother made me a costume to wear to the Mardi Gras (Fasching) celebration party with my cousin, Franz Scheller. She sewed an 1800s style officer's uniform with white and red satin, adorned with red cords and buttons on the vest. She also made a tall military cap trimmed with red rope and a feather at the top, similar to a marching band uniform. Every Mardi Gras, she meticulously made an elaborate costume for me to wear. The year before the officer uniform, I went with my father dressed as a hotel bellboy. My mother sewed the costume by hand from black satin material.

The festival commenced with a parade and electing the king and queen of Mardi Gras. My cousin Franz was a gymnast at an athletic club that organized a dance and party for Mardi Gras. I was especially excited that he asked me to go with him since I was four years younger than him.

I worked at the salon in the morning, but was allowed to leave when the parade began. I went with four girls from my trade school and we all stood along the street to watch the festivities. We had fun linking our arms together and swaying back and forth (schunkeln) to the music. We laughed and joked while we watched ornate floats travel by. We noticed one float that was nearly empty except for a caged stork bird. I don't know why a stork was in the parade, but the driver saw us having fun on the side of the street and motioned to us to hop on his float. He gave us Coke-a-Cola to drink and a bag of candy to throw to the crowds.

In the meantime, my parents were on their motorcycle driving up and down the parade route. We shouted and waved to them as they rode by us each time. My mother kept a keen eye on me as they slowly drove past our float, noticing something peculiar in my antics and laughter.

"There's something funny about the way she is acting," she said to my father.

"Oh, she's just having a good time," he said as he accelerated past our float.

My mother had a hunch that we were drunk. The driver apparently gave us beverages with alcohol and we didn't realize it. We guzzled a few bottles of coke on the float while we were singing and rocking back and forth to the music. Every time they drove by, my drunkenness became more apparent to my mother.

They stopped their motorcycle and my mother ordered me to come home with her. I told her that we didn't know there was alcohol in the coke, but she was still angry with me. I walked home with her and she sent me to bed.

That evening my cousin Franz came over to pick me up for the Mardi Gras party. I was asleep. My mother told Franz, "That little drunk is still in bed." My cousin was very upset and begged my mother to wake me up and let me go with him. After remembering all of the work it took to make my outfit, she reluctantly gave in.

"If you can wake her up she can go with you."

"Thank you, Aunt Hanni! I promise we will be good," he said.

I went to Mardi Gras in 1938 with my father, wearing a costume my mother made me as a hotel bell boy.

They roused me from my deep slumber and I dressed in my costume. My mother forced me to drink coffee and eat a sandwich before we could go. Once I looked sober, she let me leave with Franz. We had a great time dancing together and playing games at the party.

I saw the girls I drank with on the float the next day at class. They didn't realize what the driver had done either until the parade was over. We remained friends during berufschule (trade school) and enjoyed riding our bicycles together.

One afternoon, following our summer class registration, we rode our bikes to the Rhine River and stopped along the waterfront park. A wharf of stone and rocks extended out into the river and small whirlpools swirled in circles in the strong currents. A log was caught in a whirlpool as we watched it bob up and down for a long time.

One of the girls suddenly yelled, "Last one in is a rotten egg!"

Without thinking, I jumped in while no one else did. In a matter of seconds, I was caught up in a whirlpool, frantically trying to swim out. I remember struggling against the current in a panic when suddenly I felt someone's arm grab me and pull me down to the bottom of the river (to escape the whirling current). Then they pulled me out of the bottom of the whirlpool and brought me up to the surface where I swam back to the edge of the rocks. As I climbed out, I threw up water I swallowed in the struggle.

My friends patted my back while I tried to get my breath back. While everyone was looking down at me to see if I was okay, I asked, "Who saved me?"

They looked around at each other and said, "We didn't see anyone else in the water. You swam out by yourself."

"No, I didn't. I felt someone pull me out of the whirlpool," I explained.

They were bewildered, and so was I. I knew that someone had saved me yet there were no strangers around and no boats or fishermen on the river nearby that could have helped rescue me. Puzzled, I couldn't help wondering if by a miracle I was saved by a guardian angel.

CHAPTER 10

Invasion of Poland

On September 1, 1939, at the age of fifteen, I was bicycling home with some girlfriends from trade school, when one friend announced, "Did you hear on the radio that Germany declared war on Poland today?" An unsettling uneasiness spread over me as I said I had not.

"What do you think will happen next?" someone asked. We pondered the question, but nobody seemed to know.

Within weeks of the German invasion, German and Soviet forces defeated Poland by attacking from two fronts. Victory propaganda flooded our streets. Then, on September 3, 1939, Great Britain and France declared war on Germany (after a treaty agreement not to invade Poland was broken). Germany did not meet heavy resistance as they continued to invade unsuspecting countries in Western Europe, known as the Blitzkrieg.

My life didn't change much in the beginning. Most air-raid sirens were false alarms and led us to spend time in public air-raid shelters built to hold many people. Once the all-clear sounded we returned to work as usual. Although we were always apprehensive of attacks, we became accustomed to the sirens and did not rush to the shelters, even when in fact it was genuine. As the war mounted, isolated bombings and spitfire planes attacked regions we lived near. Once, I was on a train to visit my grandparents in Bremen when suddenly a plane opened fire with its machine guns on the train. I jumped off with all the passengers to shield ourselves beneath the train. Afterwards, we got back on and completed the trip as normal. Attacks usually remained isolated.

One time we were sitting in an air-raid shelter beneath our apartment building, when unexpectedly an English pilot entered our shelter. He approached with his hands up to show us he meant no harm. His plane was shot down and he was hiding. Frightened, we sat motionless. He could not speak German, but he tried to motion that he was not going to hurt us. He sat down and pulled out a picture of his wife and children to show us that he was a good man. However, no one would help him, and he finally had to surrender to the authorities as a prisoner of war.

CHAPTER 11

My Boyfriend

A few blocks away from our house sat a local tavern in Marxloh called Rosenthal. The popular pub had a band and large dance hall and I enjoyed going there with my parents. My father taught me to dance when I was a little girl. He would place me on his feet while holding me in his arms and gliding around the room to the music playing on the radio. Now that I was a teenager, my parents let me dance at Rosenthal. They didn't dance much at the tavern, instead preferring to drink and socialize with their friends. I sat with them in the lounge and they ordered me non-alcohol drinks that looked like dark beer. Once in a while a boy would ask me to dance and they gave me permission to go into the dance hall. While I danced, they sat with their friends talking and laughing all evening at my father's jokes and stories. He was the comedian of the family and entertained everyone with his sense of humor.

When I was fourteen years old, I met a young man named Franz Gesenhaus at the dance hall. He was very tall and handsome, with the longest, black lashes I ever saw on a boy. He came to Rosenthal with his friend, Paul, following work at the bakery in Marxloh. He was very polite and danced well.

Paul asked me to dance too, but he was an arrogant boy and I quickly felt dislike for him. I tried to avoid him by talking with Franz, but he kept asking me to dance. Franz intervened on my behalf. "Show some respect for Frauline Schick! She said she doesn't want to dance," he insisted. And, from that moment on Franz and I became good friends.

He was five years older than I, Roman Catholic, and very mature. He lived in Alt (Old) Walsum, a town northwest of Marxloh. He had two sisters; the oldest was a nun at a monastery in Holland. He was well-read on the scriptures and conformed to the views of the Catholic Church, valuing strong morals and principles.

By the time I was fifteen years old he had given me advice on everything, including sex and marriage. "Don't let a boy tempt you into having sex before marriage," he emphasized. "Boys will tell you they love you for sex and then leave you afterwards."

"How do you know so much?" I asked.

"My sister is a nun and sees many unwed girls with babies at the monastery," he said.

This prompted visions of helpless girls and babies without fathers to care for them in my mind, ingraining an indelible impression that I never forgot as I matured into a young woman.

By 1941, Germany had overrun most of Europe and was invading Russia. Most of the boys from town were drafted into Hitler's army and it wasn't long before Franz received his notice for the military. He began to show more interest in me and walked me home from the salon in the evenings to talk with me. He asked me if I would write to him. Being best friends, I assured him that I would write. He gave me a kiss farewell when he said good-bye.

I wrote letters to him often, and he sent me letters with pencil sketches drawn on them. He did not say much in his letters, rather conveying his feelings through his sketches. He drew a soldier sitting on a rock with a mile stone marker written on it. The soldier was looking into the distance imagining a girl writing a letter while rocking in her wicker chair. That girl was me; I realized that he was always waiting for my next letter.

Nearly one year later, when I was seventeen, he came home on his first furlough. I was at the dance sitting with some boys and girls when I glanced around the room and saw Franz sitting at a table across from me. I blurted out his name, "Franz?" He laughed and smiled at me as he got up from his chair and gave me a big hug.

"Franz, I didn't know that you were coming home," I said excitedly.

"I wanted to surprise you," he said with a big smile. "I wasn't sure if you would be here tonight," he added. It was a wonderful surprise, and we spent the evening talking and reminiscing like the old times. I missed him, and it was good to have him back home again. He was my best friend and I adored him and looked up to him like a big brother.

He was on furlough for a week and I could sense that his feelings were changing a little romantically towards me. I was now a young woman of seventeen, and he showed me a picture taken of his jeep that had my name, "Leni," painted on it. Although he didn't say it, I knew that this was his way of showing me that I was "his girl." I was very flattered and eagerly showed the picture to my friends and family.

He met me after I got out of work and walked me home. He voiced concerned for my well-being during the war and spoke candidly about the future. Although we did not have a romantic relationship, he began to behave more like a boyfriend. He wanted to spend his time with me and he kissed me with a swift peck on the lips when we said goodnight.

When he left, I began writing unknown soldiers in the war. Writing was one of my favorite pastimes since there wasn't much else to do. Once I had a silly idea to write a letter pretending to be a nine-year-old girl. I don't know why, but I sent it to an unknown soldier in the same battalion that Franz was in. I made the mistake of saying that my Uncle Franz was there too.

Franz found out about it when a soldier came up to him and said, "Hey, Franz, your niece wrote me a letter!"

"What? I don't have a niece!" he said. The soldier showed him the letter and Franz realized it was me, but thought it was the funniest thing I ever did. I was so embarrassed when he told me, and he signed his letter to me, "Uncle Franz."

I wrote other soldiers too, and sometimes they wanted to meet me when they were on furlough. My mother opened my mail and always read the letters before I got to them. One day, I received a letter from an unknown soldier who included a picture of himself. When I got home my mother showed me the picture. He was a German flyer with unattractive, big ears. My mother thought it was a funny picture. I decided to meet the young man on his furlough. His personality was just as unattractive as his looks, so I never wrote back to him again.

The friendship between Franz and I continued to grow and we were great pen pals during the war. He sketched a picture of a soldier and a girl in every letter—representing us. In one picture, he sketched himself in warfare fighting from the trenches of Russia on one side of the paper. On the other side he sketched of me with a frightened look as bombs were dropping from the sky.

He continued to use pictures in his letters to convey his thoughts. I felt his yearning to be together when he drew a boy and a girl standing with their arms outstretched trying to reach each other, but there was a war scene between them that kept them apart.

On May 30, 1943, a week before my nineteenth birthday, he returned home on furlough. It had been two years since the last time he was home. It was a Sunday afternoon when I arrived home from swimming at the local Olympic size pool at a school in Duisburg. My mother greeted me at the door with a big smile on her face and said, "Somebody you know is waiting to see you." She pointed to the other room. I walked through the room with suspicion and said, "Hello?" but he was hiding behind the door and I didn't see him. When I turned around, he flung the door shut and said, "Surprise!" I bounced up into his arms and he embraced me affectionately for the first time. I knew then that he came home for me.

He said that he would be on furlough for two weeks and he asked me if I would like to meet his parents. They lived in Old Walsum, several kilometers away. We would need to take the streetcar to get there. My hair was still wet from swimming and I wanted to style my hair and change my clothes first. He went home to give me time to get ready. He gave me directions and told me that he would meet me at the corner near his house where the streetcar stopped. This way, he had an opportunity to speak to his parents first before I arrived. It was important to me that I was dressed properly before I met his family. In those days, proper introductions were very important and it signified that he was serious about me.

He picked me up as planned and I met his parents, sister, and her boyfriend at their home. His mother asked me if I was Catholic and seemed very pleased that I was. I did not stay long because I had to return home before dark. Franz remained with his family for a few days and then traveled to Holland to visit his older sister, who lived at the monastery. He told me that he would be back for my nineteenth birthday on the following Tuesday, June 8, 1943.

When I came home from work on my birthday, I entered the house to the surprise of hundreds of flowers and bouquets decorating the floor and tables. Enthralled by the beautiful flowers, I just stood at the door in disbelief that they were for me for a while. Our house looked like a florist shop with arrangements of tulips, daffodils, hyacinths, and roses in every color and hue imaginable. Franz had packed and brought back bundles of flowers from Holland to give to me for my birthday. He and my mother unpacked them while I was at work to surprise me when I got home. Nothing made him happier than to see the expression on my face when I walked into the room. I was completely overwhelmed. He shouted, "Happy birthday!" and embraced me affectionately. He made me feel very special and he stayed with us that evening to eat strawberry shortcake that my mother made.

Later, after he left, my mother and father sat down with me and told me that he asked them if he could marry me. He was respectful of their feelings and wanted their approval before he proposed to me. They wanted me to know how they felt before he spoke to me privately. "We told him that you were our only daughter, and that we wouldn't be able to give you a proper engagement party until after the war. We suggested that you should wait to get married until he was home from the war," they explained. Most traditional engagement parties were an elaborate affair, similar to planning a wedding reception and we were living on war rations.

The next day he walked me home from work, and told me that he was considering proposing marriage to me and wanted to know how I felt about it. Because my mother had already expressed her feelings to me, and I agreed with her; I told him that we should wait until the war was over—when we could be together. He understood my feelings and said he would wait for me. Although we did not get engaged, we made a promise to each other that when he returned from the war, we would get married.

If he had proposed with an engagement ring, I might have married him, even without the engagement party that my mother wanted. But, I hadn't really thought about getting married to him before then. He had always been my best friend, and even though we knew each other for a long time, I did not know if it was true love. I never knew him romantically, but we were taught that in a good marriage you are friends first during courtship and the rest comes later.

While he was still on his furlough he wanted to visit his aunt and uncle in the country, and he asked me to go with him. We decided to travel on Sunday and ride our bicycles. It was a half a day ride and we needed to leave early in the day. But his mother told him, "Don't forget to go to church before you leave." Franz respectfully told her that we would go even though he knew that we wouldn't have sufficient time to get there if we went to church first. But he didn't want to lie to his mother, so we went inside the church for a few minutes, turned around and left to keep his promise!

By the time we arrived in the country it was getting late in the day. His aunt and uncle were excited to see Franz and me, and invited us to stay for dinner. They owned a farm and raised a few cows and goats. They asked us to stay the night, so we wouldn't have to ride our bicycles back in the dark.

We slept in separate bedrooms that night at the farm. The next morning, Franz and I went for a walk and he confessed his thoughts to me, "I almost came to your room last night," he said.

"What?" I chuckled. "After all of the things you've taught me, what makes you think that I would have let you into my bedroom?" I teased him playfully.

We both laughed about it and walked back to the farmhouse to say farewell to his relatives before our bike ride back home.

On the last day of his furlough I spent the day at his parent's house to be with him. We went for a walk together in the countryside and stopped in an area to sit and talk. He took off his jacket and laid it across the grass for us to sit on. We talked about our future. He told me he wanted to own a bakery when the war was over. He wanted to marry me someday, and he looked forward to the day that the war was over and we could be together always.

We got up and walked back to the house. His mother had a suspecting look on her face when she noticed that there was some dried grass sticking to his jacket and she brushed it off. I had a feeling that she thought we did something wrong in the grass, but she never mentioned it.

We went to the train station in Duisburg that evening, and he asked me to wait for him, ensuring me that the war would be over soon. We hugged each other for the last time. He lifted his pack over his shoulder and boarded the train.

I stood on the platform and waited for the train to depart. It was crowded with young men waving from the windows to their families and girlfriends. Franz found a seat on the train by a window and leaned through it to see me. As he waved to me, another solider next to him yelled out of the window at me, "Don't worry he'll be back for you!" he shouted.

A few weeks passed without a letter from Franz. I was at work when his father came by to tell my mother that Franz was killed in Russia. My mother was so upset. She didn't have the heart to tell me while I was still working and waited until I came home. His father told her that his battalion was in the front lines of the battlefields in Russia on July 13, 1943 in Belgorod, Russia, near the Ukrainian border. Franz was in a foxhole eating his rations, when he decided he was still hungry and he climbed out of the hole to get some more food. He was hit by shrapnel and killed.

I was overwhelmed to lose him, and to lose the dreams we made together. Although I mourned the loss of my dearest friend, I recovered from the grief of his death more quickly than I think other couples truly in love would have. I was only nineteen, resilient, and ready to move on with my life.

My neighbor kindly shared her condolences with me and asked me if I would like to have my fortune read. I sat with her as she spread her deck of cards and studied them for a few moments. She acknowledged that the cards pointed to a death of someone close to me, but she was puzzled by something in the spread of the cards. It showed that I would be getting a letter from the person who died. We began to wonder if Franz was captured and not dead. She also told me that I would be living very far away someday.

A couple weeks passed by and I received a letter from Franz, as she told me I would. He had written it just before he was killed and it took several weeks to arrive. It was the first letter that he ever expressed his true affection for me.

This photo of me was taken by my Uncle August in 1943 when I was nineteen years old.

CHAPTER 12

Trip to Zell Vineyards

In the fall of 1943 I was invited to visit Zell, Germany for some fun and relaxation to renew my spirits again. I had a friend at work, Gretchen, whose Aunt, lived in Zell, and she asked me to stay with them. It was a peaceful region known for its wine vineyards and Zeller Schwartze Katz (Black Cat) wine cellar nestled along the steep banks of the Moselle River.

My parents encouraged me to go on vacation while I still had an opportunity to enjoy life. Although Germany was at war, the frequency of Allied attacks was still sporadic, and Zell sat deep in the countryside in southern Germany.

I boarded a train in the early morning to Zell with a window seat for the journey. The train traveled on a scenic route south along the Rhine River and Moselle River, passing through regions of Germany famous for its Riesling wines. The view of the rivers meandering between the beautiful hill countries was breathtaking. Terraced vineyards grew on the steep hillsides further than the eyes could see. Ancient castles stood majestically overlooking the valleys, sparking my imagination of medieval stories and a fable I learned as a little girl about the Loreley.

The Loreley is a steep rock rising high on the bank of the Rhine River that is very difficult to navigate. A fairy-tale was written about a beautiful maiden called Loreley, sitting on the rock, combing her long, golden hair. She sings a melody, enticing

The Loreley is a steep rock in the bend of the Rhine River in the middle of the Rhine Valley, giving inspiration for the written fable of the Loreley.

the sailors with her song—and to their death against the cliff of the Loreley.

It was a cool, bright day in early autumn when my train arrived to Zell early in the afternoon. Gretchen and several young people were there to greet me. The group included young men on furlough and their girlfriends, as well as the burger mister's son from the Zeller, Schwartze Katz.

They wanted to show me around the market in the center of town to see the fountain and emblem of the Zell's Black Cat. It had its back arched and paws outstretched. This signified a fable of a black housecat that guarded a barrel of Zeller wine and ignored the barrels of other winegrowers in the cellar. The merchants presumed that the Zeller wine was very special since the cat only protected the Zeller wine barrels.

We stood around the fountain listening to the burger mister's son tell us how they grew the grapes on the steep hillsides in a soil of stony slate. It absorbed the heat of the sun during the day and released the warmth in the evening to protect the grapes from nightly frost. We were having a wonderful time talking when he asked us if we wanted to go down into the winery and taste wine from the barrels.

He led us down a flight of stairs to the entrance of the cellar. It was cool and dark inside with many large barrels of wine from many local vineyards. He gave us each a small glass to sample each

The city of Zell is on the banks of the Moselle River. Steep vineyards of grapes grew on the hillsides.

vintage. Some of the barrels were still aging and not ready for bottling, but he let us sample them right from the tap of the barrel. I had never been to a winery before and I was unaware that the group was only tasting the wine from each barrel and not drinking them. Instead of dumping my samples into a bucket, I drank them all.

When the wine tasting was over we headed back up the stairs to leave. I felt fine as we reached the top step, but when the door opened to the warm air and bright sunshine against my face I passed out!

The last thing I remembered was the warmth of the sun shinning in my face. I woke up lying in a bed in the night with the moon shinning through a small window. I didn't know where I was or how I got there. The most embarrassing moment was having to face the family and aunt who so kindly offered to let me visit.

In the morning Gretchen pulled up the blackout shades covering some of the windows to lighten the room. I humbly apologized for overdrinking and finally met her Aunt who had invited me to come. In my embarrassment, I tried to explain what had happened and she accepted my apology and welcomed me with a hug to Zell.

I spent the afternoons with Gretchen and her friends hiking up the vineyards, and exploring the old ruins of a fortress in the

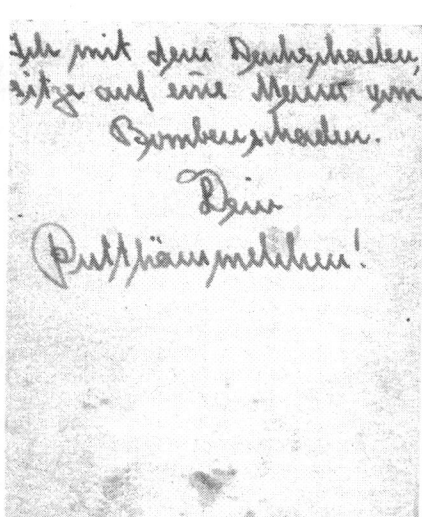

This photo was taken in 1943 as I pose against a wall damaged by a bomb. I wrote about it on the backside of the photo.

hillsides. It was a quiet wine town, and a wonderful retreat from the increasing threats of air raid attacks occurring back home. Once I returned to Duisburg, it became unsafe to travel around the country anymore.

CHAPTER 13

Air Raids of 1944

In the summer of 1944, air strikes intensified in Germany as Allied forces advanced through Europe following the U.S., British, and Canadian invasion on the beachheads of Normandy, France on June 6, 1944 (D-Day).

The Normandy invasion lasted nearly a month before the Allied forces broke through the lines of defensives that enabled them to move forward to liberate northern France and advance through northwestern Europe.

Germany's synthetic oil factories, coal refineries, and steel mills located along the Rhine River were primary targets of Allied forces to halt further production of fuel and supplies for the German forces.

We lived in Marxloh, a northern district of Duisburg near the refineries in the Bruckhausen district where my father worked. It was one of the largest industrial areas in Germany with major shipping ports on the Rhine River and rail systems for transporting fuel and war supplies.

Frequent air raid sirens sounded day and night as Allied bombers flew missions over Germany. The civilian casualties mounted. We learned that my Aunt Maria's son, Albert Scheller, who was a year younger than I, was captured by American troops after he made his first parachute jump into the Western front. He

Love, War & Curling Irons

became a prisoner of war (POW) and his family wouldn't know what became of him until the war was over.*

It became apparent that Germany's defensives had broken down and Hitler was losing the war, regardless of the propaganda, newspapers, and radio broadcasts.

One night while I rested in bed, feeling mentally and physically exhausted, the sirens went off again. It was an unsettling, nerve-racking sound, and the thought of having to go back down to the dark, cold shelter again depressed me. My parents had heard the sounds of artillery and bomb blasts in the distance and quickly yelled up to me to come down to the basement. I'm sure that I said I was coming, but I was so tired of war I thought, "If this is the end, so be it." I stayed in bed.

I don't think I slept very long when loud artillery and explosions outside suddenly awakened me. I jumped up to see what it was and saw a plane flying by my window! Engulfed in flames, the plane skimmed closely over the rooftops of the buildings. I was so frightened that I don't remember what I did next. It wasn't until the artillery fire and plane crash was over that I heard my parents calling for me, desperately trying to find me. I yelled back saying that I was under my bed and I couldn't get out from underneath it! The bed frame was so low to the floor that they were astonished to find me there.

My father lifted the bed up to get me out while my mother grasped my hands to lift me up to my feet. I was terrified, and my parents had risked their lives by leaving the safety of the shelter to find me. We rushed back to the shelter and afterwards, I never again hesitated when the sirens sounded.

---

* For the duration of his capture, he was sent to an American POW camp in Wisconsin. He worked on a farm owned by a German speaking family who became friendly with him.

Our home survived several bombing attacks throughout the war, until October 1944. We lived in a brick apartment building on the second floor. Our apartment complex was one of several three-story buildings that lined an entire city block. A courtyard and common area for the residents sat in the center of the buildings. A cement driveway for parking horse-drawn buggies, bicycles, and motorcycles curved between each apartment building. The reinforced bomb shelters were constructed below each driveway, providing good protection from air raids and collapsing buildings. Each building had a cellar below it, built with bricks. Every connecting wall had a section of bricks that did not have mortar between them so as to provide a possible escape path to the next cellar. The bricks could be pushed out if necessary to prevent being trapped inside.

Early in the war, my aunt, the wife of my father's brother Jup, died in a house fire when she was trapped beneath it in their shelter following an incendiary bombing attack. We heard her screams from the street, and although everyone desperately tried to save her, it became hopeless to reach her. My Uncle Jup lived with his daughter Martha after that tragedy. In addition to his grief of losing his wife, their son Joseph was killed in the war two weeks earlier.

On the 14th of October, my father rode his bicycle to work at the Augustissen-Hutte refinery in Bruckhausen as usual, and my mother was home alone. I left early in the morning to walk to the beauty shop. It was a straight walk down our street, Hagedorn Street, to reach Werner Ihnen's establishment on Wilhelm Street, about five blocks away. I was the oldest employee working with two younger girls and a young boy, all still apprentices in the shop. I helped in the barbershop since most of the young men were drafted into the war. I was licensed as a barber and beautician and

I could cut men's hair as well as shave their beards with a straight razor.

I had just opened the salon and slipped my apron on over my dress when the air raid sirens suddenly went off. Very orderly we shut things down and made our way down to the cellar to prepare for the air raid. I released the large latch on the cellar door and turned the handle to open the shelter door. I leaned and pressed against it heavily with my shoulder to push it open. With the door secured behind me, I entered the shelter through a second door. The space between the two doors created an air cushion, reducing the immense pressure created by explosions and shock waves of bombs. Our shelter provided good protection as long as it wasn't a direct hit.

Nervously, we huddled together, listening for warplanes flying over us. We had no idea that Duisburg would be completely destroyed by bombers that day in a wave of attacks known as Operation Hurricane.[1]

Since I was the oldest hairdresser, I tried to calm the younger students by huddling closely to them as the bombing campaign began. We could hear everything above us. The pounding of bombs, one after another, shook the ground sending tremors of fear and terror through me. Clutching tightly to each other, we winced at the sound of the whistling bombs, which sounded all too close. My boss started playing his accordion during the air raid to try and get our minds off of the loud bombing. He played some German songs that we knew and made us sing along. Then, our building suddenly shook violently above us and we knew that the

---

[1] "On October 14, 1944 in a daylight operation RAF Bomber Command sent 1,013 aircraft, with RAF fighters providing an escort, to bomb Duisburg. 957 bombers dropped 3,574 tons of high explosives and 820 tons of incendiaries on the city." Retrieved from: Wikipedia free encyclopedia. http://en.wikipedia.org/wiki/Operation_Hurricane_%281944%29.

strike must have hit part of it. The raid continued in waves above us until finally the sounds started fading into the distance, like the passing of a rumbling thunderstorm. We waited with uncertainty for the all-clear siren to sound, and then slowly returned upstairs.

The hair salon was on the first floor of the building and Mr. Ihnen's apartment was on the second. He was living by himself while his wife and young daughter were staying at a farm away from the city for safety. I felt a responsibility to help him and respected him deeply. The salon did not look damaged so he rushed up the winding iron staircase to the second floor, and yelled down to me to come up and help him. His apartment was destroyed and unlivable now with a missing wall and ceiling exposed to the sky. He needed me to help him clear out what was left and instructed his apprentices to clean the downstairs, while we carried the heavy items down the steps. We didn't stop until it was done.

A week later Mr. Ihnen remarked that my strength was superhuman that day. I helped him carry the heavy gas stove all the way down the stairs! The amazing part about it was that I didn't remember doing it and it was impossible for me to pick it up later.

I began to worry about my mother and I wanted to go home. I hurried out the door and was frightened at the sight of the devastation. Entire streets and buildings were demolished and still burning with heavy smoke from incendiary firebombs. As I reached our neighborhood, only five blocks away, I stood in disbelief as bodies were being pulled out of the rubble and laid out by the street. I wondered if my mother was alive. I looked at the bodies to see if I recognized anyone and I saw a woman with dark hair that looked like her. I was trembling and panicking as I wiped my eyes with my sleeve and looked closer at her, finally realizing it was someone else.

I screamed out for my mother. I finally found her attending to our neighbors and trying to save things from the building. She climbed over the rubble to reach me. Immediately I clung to her, pulling her as close as could be, and in my relief I didn't want to let her go.

Our apartment was still burning and smoldering from the bombing and it wasn't safe to go inside. But my mother wanted her clock and she ran back in despite the danger. She managed to get it off the wall and carried it down to the cellar. It was a German clock made of oak with beveled glass in the door. My parents bought it after they were married in 1921, and she cherished it dearly. The cellar wasn't very big so they couldn't put too much down there. They could only store the most important things, including my father's homemade alcohol.

The entire city crumbled as the unforgiving flames continued to burn throughout the city. My father managed to escape the burning refinery he worked at and came home to find us. I remember the relief in his eyes when he saw that we were okay. We felt lucky to be alive. Though we lost most of our possessions we still had each other; that was all that mattered at the time.

In the evening, after the fires and heat started to cool down in our building, my father ventured in to see if his homemade bottles of liquor were still there. He had been distilling his own alcohol for months and he was saving a batch to drink for my parents' twenty-fifth wedding anniversary party they were planning to throw on November 1, 1944. He had a homemade distiller in the kitchen and I remember watching the alcohol drip into a bottle when he brewed it. He made schnapps and liqueurs using different grains and fermented fruit he bought or traded for. I remember him testing the alcohol by lighting a small amount with a match. If it flamed, he would smile and say, "Ya, that's a good batch!" The fires from the air raid destroyed the distiller, but the bottles survived in the basement. Later that night he brought up the alcohol and said to my mother, "Let's celebrate our anniversary tonight!" So we did. He offered his distressed neighbors a drink to cheer them up too, and we sat in a broken down street car singing and joking with my father as he rang the bell on the street car pretending to be the conductor. Like a child on the playground, he made us laugh and cry until the last drop of schnapps was gone.

After the bombing we had nowhere to sleep, so we went to the hair salon where I worked and asked Werner Ihnen if we could sleep there. My boss knew my family very well since I had started at his salon as an apprentice at 13 years of age. He was happy to help us out and let us sleep on the floor in the salon that night. The next day he suggested that we move into his basement, while he slept in the back of the salon since his wife and daughter were staying in a safer district in the countryside with their relatives. We accepted his offer and returned to our bombed-out apartment to get our personal belongings stored in the cellar.

My mother had stored items such as a feather pillow, blanket, needlework, crocheted doilies, clothes, photographs, documents, and their wall clock that we carried back to the salon. However, my father's motorcycle was destroyed, disappointing him dearly. He found some scrap wood to make a bed platform from, and wooden slats to use for the top to lay the blankets onto. It became the bed that the three of us slept together in for the next eight months.

We never returned to our destroyed apartment building after that, nor did my father go back to work in the factory. I continued to work at the salon. The building didn't have electricity or gas, but I still gave men haircuts and shaves, and styled women's hair. The other apprentices returned to the salon later to continue their studies under Mr. Ihnen, but most of the time they could only practice styling hair on manikin heads. My mother came upstairs while I was working, because it was too gloomy in the basement. She sat in the back of the salon and mended socks or crocheted if she had thread.

Many buildings, unsafe after the wartime destruction, continued to topple over. Some families lived in dangerous, unstable structures that were once their homes, because they had nowhere else to go. One such building, directly across the street from the salon, stood precariously with crumbling bricks falling on the sidewalk below.

Each morning I opened up the salon for business by pulling up the wooden blinds and hanging up the "open" sign in the window. It was disheartening to look out at what was once a thriving neighborhood of merchants and shops, now just empty ruins of ragged bricks and mortar. A young woman walked by every morning and waved to me as I opened the salon. One morning, I pulled up the window blind and saw her on the other side of the street just as the entire wall of the unstable building collapsed on top of her. The sudden crash of bricks startled me so much that I let go of the rolling blind just in time as the bricks slammed into our building, hitting the window where I stood. The window blind provided protection from the flying debris and I did not get hurt. Many people came running in an attempt to rescue the woman across the street, but she was crushed by the tremendous weight of the bricks.

There was a little nook in the back of the salon with a sitting area and potbelly stove for heat and cooking. It had a flat surface on top to warm up a pot of water or soup. Otherwise, in order to have a meal, my parents stood in long lines to get some food or supplies with their rations stamps. These were coupons that we would redeem for food. Every family was issued ration stamps throughout the war based on the size of their family and ages of their children. The stamps could be used to get basic necessities such as bread, butter, sugar, jelly, canned meat, and coffee. However, the food supplies would run out and my parents often came back without anything. We stood in long soup lines with a bowl, cup, pot, or any container we had to put food into. They used a large soup ladle to fill our bowl with stew or soup and sometimes they gave us a piece of bread.

I saved the money I made between 1938 and 1944 in the bank, but to get goods we had to use our ration coupons. In addition to food rations, each family usually got a ration for a pair of shoes, socks, or other essentials maybe once or twice during the war. That is why we mended our socks over and over again until there was more mending than sock. We couldn't buy clothes, so we would take apart the clothes we had and make something else from them. It gave us something to do and made us feel better about ourselves. We were still able to get some money out of the bank to buy some things we couldn't get with ration coupons. Sometimes at the salon we would overhear customers talking about where to go to get flour, coffee, cigarettes, or a loaf of bread being sold on the black market. I would spend some of the money I had to buy my parents chocolate, or anything special that we couldn't buy elsewhere. Life went on, and everyone else lived in the same type of conditions as us. There was always someone worse off than us, and we were grateful for what we had.

Werner Ihnen's wife and daughter were living at a farm about 150 kilometers away in the country for safety. He thought that it would be safer for them to live in the country than in the city. They stayed in a shed next to a farmhouse throughout 1944. His young daughter of three was by herself in the shed when a war plane flew over. It was believed that a pilot was probably going back home from a mission and released his bomb before returning to base over open fields. Unfortunately, the bomb struck the shed, killed their child, and damaged the farmhouse. It was a sad, isolated incident that the pilot may not have ever known about. After Mr. Ihnen heard the sorrowful news, his wife returned home.

My mother became restless and worried about her parents safety in Bremen, and she knew that they were worried about us too. Communication wasn't possible and it made her sullen and depressed as the war continued into 1945.

We sat many evenings reminiscing about the summers I traveled by train to Bremen to stay with my oma and opa. They taught me to be independent and self-reliant at an early age; I did not have any reservations about traveling on my own. I knew that when the war was over, I would seek them out.

CHAPTER 14

Germany Surrendered

In the spring of 1945, several months after the invasion of Normandy, the Allies advanced further into Germany forcing the German's to retreat. By May 3rd, the German forces surrendered in Denmark, Holland, and North Germany, with an unconditional surrender signed on May 7, 1945. Victory in Europe Day (V-E Day) was celebrated May 8th, although other nations and territories remained occupied by German forces. Eventually, the remaining areas under German occupation all surrendered, with complete peace on May 11th.

The evening before the Allies took occupation of Duisburg, my parents and I were in the basement of the salon when we heard a commotion above us on the street along with the sound of troops scuffling their boots as they walked by. We clamored quickly up the stairs, and out of a window saw the young, weary faces of German soldiers, including boys as young as 13 years old, retreating hastily from the Allies.

"Germany has surrendered!" They shouted. "Be prepared to surrender tomorrow morning when they take-over the city," they warned. Soon they were out of sight, and we waited for morning with fear and uncertainty about our future.

We lay awake that night, anticipating our country's fate. Neighbors watched the night sky for signs of resistance. Yet, the city remained quiet and untouched by enemy fire. Early in the morning after daybreak, we watched out the salon windows. White scarves hung from open windows and doorways of the buildings that were still standing. I saw soldiers ducking into the doorways, looking up for potential snipers. We sighted more soldiers dashing between buildings, but we never heard any shooting. Once they infiltrated the city, the trucks and tanks came rolling in. There was no confrontation during the unconditional surrender and the German people waved anything white that they had as the troops went by. Children seemed the most curious about the soldiers now occupying our city. They would gather around the soldiers and ask them for candy. The most shocking part is that some boys would try to sell their sisters for chocolate by saying, "You got chocolate? I've got sister!" The soldiers gave them some chocolate or rations if they had some, but then went on their way.

When the Allies assumed power over Germany, the western portion of Germany, where we lived, became West Germany as a democratic country. The Soviet Union occupied the zone that became East Germany under communist rule. There was no hostility or resistance under the controlling command of the Allies. The troops in charge were kind and considerate. They had been at the front lines of battle and understood the hardship and misery of war that our nations endured. Our fears and anxieties lessened as the Allies took over and governed some of the rebuilding process. They repaired and rebuilt some of the bridges and railways in order to maneuver troops and equipment to other locations. Some electrical power and gas was eventually restored.

I was able to work at the salon during the day but we had to abide by nightly curfews. Allied soldiers walked by the salon while I was working in the barbershop, and stopped in front of the window to watch us work. Others leaned on the windowsill with their elbows, fascinated to see women cutting men's hair and shaving their beards with straight razors!

CHAPTER 15

Journey to Bremen

On the 8th of June, 1945 I was turning 21 years old. Two weeks prior to my birthday I became ill with signs of a kidney infection. Painful urges to use the bedpan plagued me throughout the night as I got up to go without relief. I slept on the same makeshift bed as my parents did in the basement of the salon and I did not want to disturb them as I constantly got up. Confused and sick I returned to bed and did not get up anymore, embarrassingly flooding the entire platform they slept on.

My health worsened with fever and chills. My mother sat by my bedside feeding me home remedies of broth and soup to try and cure my infection; medical help was impossible. My mother's friends helped me by letting me stay in their home in the country. I enjoyed fresh air and peaceful rest in a soft bed, away from the damp and dark basement of the salon.

After several days of relaxation and fluids my fever broke and I began to eat, regaining my strength sufficiently to return home for my birthday.

Strawberries were in season in June, but a delicacy not found in our war-torn city. Strawberry shortcake became a birthday tradition in our family and I can't imagine the anguish my mother would have felt if she couldn't make it for me. Somehow she found the means to buy strawberries and cream to serve it on my birthday. How she managed it is not entirely clear, but it was the only gift she could give me – and it was delightful!

After my birthday I decided to go to Bremen to find my grandparents. The town, located on the Weser River, was a major port. It could have been a target of the Allies before the surrender of Germany. I was distraught by my mother's concern and worries about them. I knew I should seek them out on my own since my father had breathing problems and would not be able to endure the long journey by foot.

"I think I can make the trip in a few days," I told my parents. "I know a girl that might be able to go with me," I reassured them.

During the war I became friends with a girl named Margaret. I met her in an air raid shelter during the bombings and drills. As we chatted, we realized that our grandparents lived in the same area in the outskirts of Bremen. We said that we would travel there together one day to see if they survived the war safely. Once I made up my mind that I was going, I asked her if she was still interested. She was, and we both felt relieved that we would have each other for companionship on the long journey north.

I washed the only clothes I had, and packed them into a knapsack. My mother sewed some shoulder straps on to it so I could wear it on my back comfortably during the trip. She helped me roll up a blanket to take with me and packed it in my bag. It would be a long trip to Bremen, taking several days; I needed to carry a light load on my back. We were hoping to jump onto a train whenever there was an opportunity, so I needed my hands free to grab onto the car handrails. The trains didn't move very fast, however it took some quick maneuvers to hop on. Many people searching for their relatives would sneak into boxcars for a ride. There wasn't any other means to get across Germany except to walk. Most of the cities were bombed out, and we, like many people, wanted to find our relatives to live with them. My mother had no way of knowing if her parent's home was still standing and if they would have room for us to stay with them unless I went there in person. There were no telephones, telegrams, or mail services available, so we had to see for ourselves if they were well, traveling by any means possible.

The day we left, Margaret met me at the salon because she lived further away from the route we would take. My mother helped me secure my knapsack on my back while she spoke some final words of motherly advice to me. With a loving embrace we said good-bye and we left on our journey northward.

We decided to follow the train route leading from Duisburg to Bremen. Many train stations, bridges, and tracks were destroyed during the war, limiting the possibility of hopping onto a train. However, I was very familiar with each town along the route having visited my grandparents often as a young girl. I knew I could find my way even if we walked the entire distance. It would be nearly 300 km (186.4 mi) to reach our destination, so an early start in the morning gave us a full day of light to begin our travel.

Once we heard a train whistle, we would wait near the tracks watching for open boxcars to pass. Most boxcars were already filled with people seeking refuge from our torn country, so when we jumped onto the bumper or step of a boxcar we had to hang on outside of it. I got so dirty with smoke and soot from the engines that my face and clothes were blackened.

The conductors knew that people were jumping into the cars, so they kept most of the doors open. Sometimes the trains stopped because the tracks were bombed out and we had to get off and walk. Once, we walked over a destroyed rail bridge above the Ems River near Osnabrück with only one rail intact. We were at risk for slipping into the river below so we crawled on our hands and knees to cross more securely. It was the only option we had to cross and continue our journey.

We spotted convoys of English army trucks picking up passengers on the side roads. We joined groups of people to get a ride on the backs of the open trucks, even if it was a short trip. Once they stopped we got off and continued by foot until another convoy went by. The Allied convoys drove on local routes and could only take passengers a few kilometers. We often walked because they were not driving in the same direction we were heading.

The first night of our journey we slept in a boxcar with other people. It was June and the weather was warm in early summer. We felt comfortable and cuddled together with the blanket my mother packed for me. Many weary travelers went to sleep hungry and exhausted that night in an isolated boxcar on the tracks.

The next morning Margaret and I were famished. We met a man and a woman on a road willing to share their food with us. The kind woman opened her bundle and tore off the crust of her bread and gave it to us. People were still kind and caring even in hard times. We were so grateful and thanked them for their kindness and continued our journey north. We found a well at a farm along the way and we drew water from it to quench our thirst. Occasionally we stopped to rest and sat under a tree for shade, but our hunger propelled us to keep walking throughout the night and we did not sleep.

On the third day we came across a caravan of English army trucks stopped in a road. They were taking a break and people stood in line to climb into the back of the trucks. We motioned with our hands to get the soldiers attention and asked if we could board the truck too. A person standing in the line spoke some

English and translated our request to the soldiers. We stood in line for a while. When I got up close to the truck the driver pointed at me and signaled with his finger to come over. I walked over to the side of the truck where he stood. He looked closely at me and then took his helmet off and filled it up with water. Then he found a rag and handed it to me, motioning for me to wash my face. I cupped my hands and splashed the refreshing water on my face. It felt so good! I washed my face with the cloth he gave me, removing a layer of grime that turned the water black. I knew I must have looked awful with my face hidden under layers of black soot and it was a relief to wash it off. As I wiped my face dry and looked up at him, he smiled in delight. I don't know what he thought, but he flushed with excitement when he saw what I really looked like under all of that dirt!

The soldier arranged the mirror on his truck so I could see myself. My hair was knotted so I found a comb in my pocket and fixed it the best I could. The rest of the people were filling up the back of the truck and I couldn't see Margaret with the canvas cover over the back. I wanted to get on the back with the others, but he beckoned me with his finger to stay. He didn't have any other passengers in the cab of the truck and directed me to ride up front with him. My first thought was that there wasn't any more room in the back of the truck and that is why he wanted me to go in the front with him, so I did. When I sat down with him he got out his water canteen, k-rations, chocolate, and anything he could find in his pockets for me. He just smiled at me as I enjoyed every morsel. I was so hungry, but I felt guilty that Margaret wasn't with me. I hid some of the food in my pockets so I could give some to her later. Their unit took us into Bremen and dropped us off. I never knew his name but always remembered how nice he was to me. Margaret reacted with a little jealousy towards me, but she got over it quickly when I gave her the food I saved in my pockets.

It took us three days to get to Bremen, a distance of 300 km (186.4 mi) from Duisburg. From that point, we still had to walk further northwest of the city to Vegasack, nearly 24 km. (15 mi.) away. Most of Bremen's buildings and churches appeared to be unscathed by bombing compared to Duisburg. Streetcars were running in some sections, and if Margaret and I would have had any geld (money), we would have taken one. Instead we walked to Vegasack and then continued another 2 km. (1.2 mi.) to Aumund, the village where my grandparents lived. Upon arriving, we embraced and said farewell. She continued on, walking to Blumenthal, 5.4 km (3.4 mi) west, to find her relatives. I walked to my grandparents house a short distance away. I never saw or heard from her again.

CHAPTER 16

I Reach Oma's House

After three exhausting days traveling to Aumund, I looked for my grandparents' street, but did not recognize the area. Most of the familiar landmarks I knew were gone, including the heavily wooded areas surrounding the community that I used to walk through as a child. Winters were bitterly cold in northern Germany, and any source of fuel for heat was squandered quickly.

Fond memories of my childhood vacations rushed through my mind as I grew more anxious to get to my grandparents' house. From across a field I saw the old brick house just as I remembered it—two stories high and still unscathed by the war. I couldn't contain my excitement any longer; I ran the rest of the way. I paused momentarily at the gate of their front yard, thrilled with jubilation as my journey came to an end. I saw Oma tending to her small garden beside the house. She didn't see me approaching when I burst out her name, "Oma!"

She looked up in astonishment and dropped her garden tools to the ground to hug me. Ecstatically she repeated, "You are here! You are here!" while she embraced me tightly to her bosom in a joyful reunion.

"Opa, come here quickly! Leni is here!" she exclaimed.

He rushed out of the kitchen door to greet me and anxiously asked if my parents were alive and well. I reassured them that they were safe and staying with Werner Ihnen at the salon in Duisburg while my friend, Margaret and I journeyed by foot to get here.

"You must be starving, you poor child," she said. "Let's go into the house so I can make you something to eat!"

The aroma from the smoke house tantalized my senses as she went inside of it and cut off a piece of sausage and smoked ham to bring to the kitchen.

"Sit my dear, you look famished!" she said as she sliced the meat and bread to make me a sandwich. While I ate, we talked about all of the tragic events that had taken place in Duisburg, and how my mother and father were worried about them. I told her that we lost everything we had and that my parents wished to move in with them if they had room for us.

"Of course we have room!" she said with tears welling up in her eyes. "Don't worry, we will send for them," she said. Then, we spent the rest of the day talking about the rest of the family and about her unusual new friend, an American soldier.

My grandparents were fortunate that most of the homes and buildings in Aumund were spared during the war. Since I was a child I always remembered my grandparents living in the same house. In their four-bedroom house they raised three girls and three boys: August, Martha, Johanne, Emil, Elli, and Karl. It never had bathroom plumbing or running water. Instead, it had an outhouse built in the back of the house with two seats in it. Water was retrieved from the well outside that the neighbors shared. The well had two buckets that were lowered and raised by a crank handle. Once the filled buckets were raised to the top they would have to be poured into other buckets to carry home.

Oma and Opa raised chickens and geese for food, including a pig my opa raised in a small pen in the backyard. He would purchase a piglet each year and raise it until it was ready for slaughter. The meat would then be cured in a smokehouse he built behind the house. Oma tended to their garden everyday growing vegetables and flowers along the side of the house. She canned the vegetables and cut fresh flowers that she displayed in the house. They had a small garden house in the middle of the garden and Opa and his friends would sit in it to play a game of cards or sip a bottle of schnapps sometimes.

Weeks before I arrived at my grandparents' house, American troops, stationed in northern Germany, provided food rations to the German people. Fred Grehl was an American sergeant stationed in Blumenthal to oversee deliveries and distribution of food to a designated area on the edge of town. They loaded leftover scraps and food from the army mess hall onto a truck for delivery. Fred was an interpreter for the army, speaking directly with the German people. When they made their daily deliveries, he kept order and handed out the food rations to the crowds. The food disappeared quickly, and he did his best to satisfy everyone.

Each day, Opa would take his milk can in the wagon to the distribution area to try and get it filled with some scraps for his pig. But, he never got anything because all the other people would get in front of him. One morning, he left the house late and the truck drove by him as he was pulling his wagon. Fred recognized him and stopped the truck to talk to him. He felt bad that the old man usually didn't get any food. Since Fred was fluent in German he politely asked, "What do you need?"

Opa replied, "I have a pig and I need some scraps to feed him." Fred had one of his men fill up his milk can and told him that from then on he would stop at his house each day and drop off some scraps for his pig first so that he wouldn't have to pull his wagon all the way to the edge of town anymore. Fred kept his promise and stopped the truck everyday as they drove down his street, giving him first choice of anything they had. My grandparents became very fond of him, and loved to talk with him and learn of his German heritage. Fred seemed to be just as enthusiastic as they were to visit each day. He told my oma that they reminded him of his parents who emigrated to the U.S. from Germany in 1923. He told her how he missed his parents and sisters very much, and Helene and August felt like family to him. He often stopped by after his deliveries to visit and bring them something special to eat or drink, especially coffee. Oma enjoyed making him a pot of coffee or dessert and chatting with him. She said she even made him strawberry shortcake one time from their strawberry patch. They shared a wonderful relationship that would continue to grow and endure.

This is a photo of my grandparents, Helene and August Göhner in Bremen-Aumund. Behind them is a tool shed on the backside of the house. Oma was born April 5, 1874 and my grandparents were married in 1893.

CHAPTER 17

The American Soldier

The evening I arrived to my grandparents' house, Oma couldn't stop talking about her American friend.

"Oma, how can you talk to an American soldier?" I asked.

"He speaks German fluently," she said. "He is an interpreter," she added.

She described his kindness and thoughtfulness and told me how he visited them daily, delivering scraps for Opa's pig. He had done many favors for them without them ever asking and they wanted me to meet him in the morning.

After supper, I washed up and slipped into one of Oma's soft flannel nightgowns to go to bed. I crawled under the covers and sunk my weary head into a cushion of soft down feather pillows atop a feather mattress so comfortable it felt like I was sleeping on a cloud. Oma came into my room to tuck me in like she did when I was a little girl. She snuggled beside me and rubbed my back tenderly as I drifted to sleep, the deepest sleep I had in many months.

I was savoring the first time sleeping in a real bed since our house was destroyed, and I didn't want to get up when Oma shook my arm and woke me the next morning.

"Leni, the American truck is outside! Come out to the gate to meet my American boyfriend!"

I quickly got up, dressed, and combed the tangles from my hair, then joined my grandparents outside. The truck was parked in front of their house. I watched the soldier jump off of the truck with his rifle strapped to his shoulder. He wore brown army fatigues and a helmet that he removed as he approached us with a big grin and look of curiosity. With exuberance in his voice he spoke in German saying, "Good morning!" He looked at me with excitement in his eyes, as my oma introduced him as her American friend, Fred! He began conversing with me in a surprisingly flawless German dialect and I stood there dumbfounded as he spoke. I suddenly felt awkward and attracted to this handsome man standing in front of me. His wavy blond hair, sparkling blue eyes, smile, and politeness made it difficult for me to look at him. I was very intrigued by him, yet I didn't want to show it. I could sense that he was very attracted to me too, but I played hard to get. After awhile, he had to go about his business and he left Opa some scraps for his pig, said good-bye, and mentioned that he hoped to see me later.

I didn't have any clean clothes to wear, so I walked to Aunt Ellie's home in Vegesack to see if she would let me wear some of hers. Aunt Ellie was a very stylish woman, always wearing the latest fashions. She lived in a modern apartment with running water and a hot water heater for washing and bathing. When I arrived at her door, she was overwhelmed with joy to see me. We chatted for a long time and then she let me take a bath and wash my hair. We wore the same size clothes, so we browsed through her closet to pick out some dresses and shoes I could wear. It was getting late in the afternoon, so I left to go back to my grandparents' house before it got dark.

In the meantime, Fred came back to my grandparents' house in the afternoon when he finished his deliveries, but I was not home. He asked Opa if he could come back in the evening and take me to a movie. Opa said that he couldn't speak for me and that he would have to come back later to ask me himself.

After I returned, Klonder, a friend of the family, came over to visit and help crush sunflower seeds to make oil. We were laughing and joking around when Fred came over that evening. Instead of talking to him, I just kept crushing sunflower seeds with Klonder, ignoring Fred. I was laughing and teasing Klonder when I looked around at Fred sitting across the room with a look of jealousy on his face that I will never forget. I'm sure that he was ready to stand up and leave when my opa pulled me aside and said, "If you don't be nice to that boy and talk to him, I won't get anymore food for my pig!" So, after being reprimanded by my opa, I started talking to him. He asked me very sweetly if I wanted to go to a movie in Vegasack. He said it was an American movie starring Bing Crosby called, *Going My Way*. It would be spoken in English, but he could interpret it for me. I eagerly accepted, and he told my grandparents that he would have me back by the ten o'clock curfew.

The USO set up the movies for the soldiers as a way of keeping up their morale in service. Bing Crosby was one of Fred's favorite actors and he didn't want to miss the new movie. We walked to the theater in the center of Vegasack while he carried his rifle on his shoulder. The theater was crowed with noisy soldiers and their girlfriends. We shuffled through a tight aisle to find some good seats. There was a sudden hush of silence around us as the flash of the movie projector lit the big screen.

*The American soldier,
Sergeant Fred Grehl.*

During the movie he leaned close to my ear and I could smell his aftershave as he whispered what the actors were saying to me in German. It was a delightful, lighthearted story and musical that stirred my imagination and feelings as I sat next to Fred. As the plot intensified, I curled against him and he pulled me closer to his side, giving me a heightened sense of security with his arm draped around my shoulder. His warm breath and lips touched my ear as he whispered, "Are you enjoying the movie?"

"Yes." I nodded, as a strange excitement flooded my body.

I couldn't remember a time that I had ever enjoyed more. He walked me home that evening and visited with my grandparents in the den for a while. Pulling out his harmonica from his shirt pocket, he asked us if we would like to hear some music. He delighted and surprised my grandparents and me by the number of German songs he knew so well. We had a wonderful time, and he asked me if he could see me again. I said, "Yes."

CHAPTER 18

A Night at the USO Dance

The United Service Organizations (USO) set up facilities to entertain the troops overseas one night. Fred asked me if I would like to go out dancing. The USO played swing band music at their dances on 78-rpm records by famous artists like Glenn Miller, Duke Ellington, and Tommy Dorsey (popular in the 1940s).

That evening, I wore a beautiful blue dress belonging to Aunt Ellie. Fred arrived to pick me up wearing his military uniform and hat. He was handsome and stunning in his uniform as he escorted me to the dance.

The USO provided beverages, food, and entertainment for the evening. We sat down at a table and I was introduced to all of his comrades. When the music began to play, he asked me to dance with him. His rhythm and skill was remarkably smooth as he led me around the dance floor. During slow songs, he held me close and we danced cheek-to-cheek. He knew every popular dance and taught me how to swing dance. He was the greatest dance partner I ever had; I felt like Ginger Rogers dancing with Fred Astaire.

We enjoyed several dances together, but when we sat down to the table his buddies kept asking him to translate what they were saying to their German girlfriends. They kept buying him drinks so he wouldn't stop translating for them. The bartender, Pierie Clabeaux, knew what was going on and joked around with me. He

Fred in his formal military uniform.

spoke a little bit of German, so I sat at the bar for a while with him and he offered me a couple drinks. He looked older than most of the soldiers, but I had some good laughs with him.

By the end of the evening Fred and I were quite intoxicated. It was near closing time and we had to walk back home. However, if we walked he wouldn't make it back to camp in time for curfew. His lieutenant recognized that we had too much to drink that night and he offered to drive us home in his jeep. He dropped us off at Oma's house. We stayed outside for a while, not feeling well after overdrinking. Eventually, we both threw up under the fruit trees! Fred was under a pear tree and I was under an apple tree. He had to be back to his barracks by 1:00 a.m., the curfew that night, but time was running out. He asked Oma if he could borrow her bicycle to go back. She agreed and offered it to him any time he needed it.

The next time he visited me, he told me about an American song by the Andrew Sisters with the lyrics, "Don't sit under the apple tree with anyone else but me." He sang it to me but changed the words slightly to, "Don't throw up under the apple tree with anyone else but me!" We laughed, and never forgot the words.

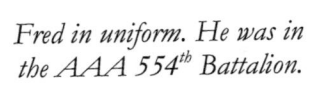

Fred in uniform. He was in the AAA 554th Battalion.

I found out later that the bartender at the USO dance was in charge of the mess hall. Afterwards, he gave Fred extra food for us and special cuts of meat to eat. Whenever he saw Fred he would call him over to the kitchen. "Here's something to take to your special girl!" he smiled.

Fred continued to deliver leftover food and scraps to the edge of town. They parked the truck near an open field to distribute to the Germans. On one particular day, the kitchen staff obtained a goat they didn't want to cook or serve to the GI's. Instead, they suggested that Fred take it with him on his delivery.

"Take the meat with you and try to barter with the people to get some good schnapps in exchange for the meat," they asked. Fine liquor was hard to come by and they pleaded with Fred to do it, and he said he would.

So that day when they stopped the truck, Fred announced, "We have fresh goat meat here that we will carve up pieces for anyone who can bring me back some hard liquor or schnapps!" Suddenly, everyone vanished as they rushed home to find some booze. Soon afterwards they all returned with a bottle to

Fred standing behind an Anti-Aircraft Artillery 40 mm weapon with his battalion. He carried this picture in his wallet throughout the war.

exchange, and Fred returned to his barracks with enough liquor to keep his battalion drunk for three days!

He came to see me every day while he was stationed in Blumenthal. He would visit in the evenings and we would talk for hours about the war and his battalion. He was an Anti-Aircraft Artillery Weapons Crewman in the 554th Anti-Aircraft Artillery AW (Automatic Weapons) Battalion, in C ("Charlie") Platoon, Battery 'B.' His tour of duty included overseeing the 40 mm gun and 6 men in combat, assigning positions to men, and the proper firing of weapons. He became acting chief of his section, in charge of 14 men and 2 guns. He was promoted to platoon Sergeant, in charge of 56 men, before the war was over. He landed on Omaha beach the day after D-Day, fighting the battles and campaigns in Normandy, Northern France, Rhineland, and Central Europe. He earned several decorations including: the American Theater Ribbon, European-African-Middle Eastern Theater Ribbon w/4 Bronze Battle Stars, 3 Overseas Service Bars, Good Conduct Medal, and the Purple Heart Medal following his shrapnel wounds received in France July 7, 1944.

Fred was homesick and missed his family. He told me about his German ancestry and how his family emigrated to the U.S. He lived in Paw Paw, Michigan, and he was in high school when he decided to quit school to enlist in the army on March 1, 1943. He joined the army so he could take care of his mother and sisters after the U.S. government detained his father, Fritz, in an American internment camp as an "enemy alien". The government did this during WWII, because he did not have his naturalization papers as a U.S. citizen. Persons of German ancestry were "watched" by the government during the onset of WWII, even if they were citizens of the country. This left his family without any income. Fred sent more than two thirds of his paycheck to his mother, Erna, to help support his family. His sister, Gisela, was married to Jimmy Sullivan, but his grandmother, Augusta Diemer, lived with his mother and sisters, speaking German only at home.

He was very open and honest when he spoke, and I felt safe and comfortable around him. We went for walks and sat in the garden house in the evenings. It was a small dwelling near the house that could accommodate up to four people comfortably and was great for an afternoon visit over a cup of coffee or tea. Fred and I would sit out there in the evenings to be alone. He called it our, "love shack" because we smooched in there! He was romantic, but he also had a playful side to him, like when he occasionally pretended to be Humphrey Bogart, an American actor in the 1940's. He would murmur in English to me in a suave, "Bogart" style and tone that mesmerized me. I didn't know what he was saying, but the way he said it swept me off my feet! It wasn't until several years later that I learned what Fred really said to me! As he looked into my eyes he said softly, "Babe, your nose runs like a bubbling brook." He never did let on to me of his mischievousness!

Family picture of the Grehl's taken around 1936. From the left are Gisela, Betty, Fritz, Erna, Fred, and Wilgard. *

---

* Fred's father, Fritz Grehl came from Kassel, Germany, immigrating to America alone in August 1923, and stayed with his sister-in-law Anna Wetzel (Ann) and her husband Dan, at 63rd Str. Chicago, Ill. (Ann immigrated to America in 1921, sponsored by her Uncle Ernst Vogt and married Dan Wetzel a U.S. citizen.) Fritz sent for Erna, eight months pregnant with Fred, and Gisela one year old. Erna's mother and brother, Auguste Diemer and William (Bill) Diemer accompanied them to America in December 1923. Her mother was a widow and lived with them after Wilhelm Diemer fell from a ladder and broke his neck. Fred was born in Chicago, Illinois, January 7th 1924, one week after his family immigrated to the U.S. in 1923.

They returned to Germany in 1932 when Fred was eight years old for five years. Wilgard was born October 26, 1934 in Germany. The family decided to move back to the U.S. Auguste Diemer returned first in August 1936. Fritz brought Fred and Betty to America on April 2, 1937, since they were natural citizens. Once settled in Chicago, he sent for Erna, Gisela, and Wilgard on June 8, 1937. Fred returned to school in Chicago at the age of thirteen.

CHAPTER 19

The Engagement Party

Fred and I fell deeply in love and our feelings for each other only grew stronger each day we were together. About a month after we met, he asked me if I would marry him. He wanted to wed in Germany and take me back to the United States with him. He went to his commander and his high officials to ask if we could get married, but he was told it wasn't allowed yet. He would be shipped out of Germany soon and going back to America. I remember the heartache and disappointment we felt. He couldn't stay in Germany and he was extremely homesick and wanted to see his family again. But, he promised that he would send for me. He wanted to get engaged as a symbol of our love and commitment, so we planned an engagement party.

All of my aunts and uncles on my mother's side lived in Bremen. We invited them to come to the house for a small engagement party to meet Fred. My mother and father, still in Duisburg, did not yet know about our engagement. Fred brought some food and coffee from the mess hall and Oma made the cake. Aunt Ellie and Aunt Marta attended, and we sat in the front room together. During the party, Fred and I exchanged rings. He wore a ring on his little finger that he gave me, and I had a ring with a garnet stone in it that I gave him. The family was overjoyed and happy for us. While Fred and I chatted with the family, my grandmother must have gone back into the kitchen to talk to my grandfather privately. She came back into the front room and said to us, "Exchanging rings just won't do! If this is supposed to be an engagement, you need an engagement ring." She then took off her gold wedding band from her finger and gave it to us. It was a very touching and sentimental moment while Fred slid the ring onto my finger and kissed me. I wore it on my left hand because it is a German custom to wear an engagement ring on the left hand until wed. Then, after marriage the ring is placed on the right hand. My family warmly congratulated us with our official engagement.

CHAPTER 20

Fred Goes Home

Before Fred was shipped out of Blumenthal he brought over extra food, sweets, and scrap food for Opa's pig. He delivered anything that he could if he thought we could use it. One day he brought over boxes and boxes of pancakes! We invited the entire neighborhood over to eat them with us.

On another occasion, he left a truckload of boxes in our yard. The lining of the boxes contained a black paper that burned well and could be used in the wood burning stove. It may have been tar paper. We folded the boxes up and stored them in the shed to burn for heat in the winter. He was always thinking of us and he didn't want us to get cold! He continued to drop off anything he possibly could to help us out before he left.

We spent three glorious months together before he got his papers to ship out back home. His love and commitment helped keep me strong as we said our final good-bye.

In September of 1945, his unit left Blumenthal for another area in Germany. He was stationed in France for a few weeks and then in England. Mail was censored by the military. In order to write to me, he would put his letter to me inside another letter to soldiers still stationed in Blumenthal. He asked his friends to bring me his letters personally. This is how we corresponded until I got his last letter saying that he was being shipped back home to the United States. He would arrive in America on October 30, 1945.

My parents did not have an opportunity to meet Fred. They arrived in Aumund two days after Fred left. They were still in Duisburg getting their belongings together to ship by freight train to Aumund and couldn't leave until they had everything shipped. When they arrived at my grandparents' house they learned of our engagement. My oma expressed her joy and approval, recounting all of the events that had taken place since I had arrived. She reassured my parents that they need not worry about us, and that they would accept him as wholeheartedly as they did.

CHAPTER 21

After the War

On September 15, 1945, I began working again. This time for a man named Franz Pulczynski, who owned a men and women's hair salon in Bremen-Aumund on Lindenstraße. It was a small salon, about one half mile from my grandparents' home. I worked with Franz and his wife. They were not as amicable as my former boss in Duisburg, so I never got to know them very well. However, working for Franz kept me busy and I earned some money again.

My father found work at a warehouse operated by the Allies, sorting and stacking garments such as shirts, pants, hats, scarves, socks, and underwear. They hired German people to organize and stock the warehouse. The army guards would check bags and frisk the workers for stolen articles each day when they clocked out. Much of the clothing was surplus for the military soldiers. My father actually pulled some "fast ones." He was so skinny, that he could put clothes on underneath his regular clothes and walk off the premises without anyone suspecting him. The guards would frisk him, but they most likely felt his ribs and not the clothes he put on underneath.

He traded the clothes for necessary essentials like butter and milk from local farmers in the area. He also traded for wheat, and took it to the mill to have it ground into flour for making bread. I remember him coming home with some sailor scarves made with fine yarn that I unraveled to make myself a pleated skirt.

Occasionally, the neighbors planned a heist to break open a boxcar containing supplies and food shipped to the Allies' warehouses. By word of mouth, we knew when a train would be cracked open. The trains traveled slowly at night around a bend curving sharply near an open field not far from where we lived. It was for those quick on their feet to open it up and throw out supplies from the boxcar to the ground.

People hid along the tracks hoping to grab something that was tossed out before the Military Police (MP) saw them. Most often, the trains carried cargos of canned food being shipped to the Allied forces stationed in Bremen.

My father was gassed during the First World War and he got out of breath easily. Due to his weak stamina he could not participate in any of these scrupulous schemes. However, I ventured out on occasion and picked up coffee and boxes of chocolate. One night, when the moon was very bright, I watched to see if any goods were being thrown from the boxcars. That particular night, heavy tin cans that weighed five or ten pounds were tossed out. I didn't know what was in them, but I ran and grabbed one. It was a big can. I raced back to our house but the moonlight was reflecting off the can and I saw the MPs headlights coming down our street. They knew that people would be trying to break into the cars and they were out in the night with their flashlights searching for suspicious activity. My heart started racing and I jumped down into the ditch in front of our house and covered the can with my body, laying as close to the ground as possible while the jeep slowly drove by. The MPs didn't detect me. Once I got into the house, my father opened it up. To his delight it contained bacon. The only other time we had bacon was when Opa slaughtered his pig each year. People like us were just trying to survive the hard times even if it was unethical.

The Military Police often searched suspecting homes for stolen goods following such events. We hid the goods atop ceiling rafters off the kitchen connecting to the porch. We discretely concealed every chocolate bar and can goods from sight.

By 1946, much of our hidden supply was given to Aunt Eli to help restore her husband's health after he was released from prison camp in Russia. Otto Hilmer arrived home on the brink of death, his body decimated from malnutrition and unspeakable mistreatment in prison. Food and care was administered to him day and night in hopes of his recovery. Our hidden can goods and chocolate candy helped save his life. He suffered from chronic diarrhea and couldn't seem to regain any weight. It was then that we began feeding him a diet of dark chocolate candy! Miraculously, the chocolate therapy worked, stopping his diarrhea and enabling him to regain his strength.

CHAPTER 22

Fred's Letter

Fred and I couldn't write each other for over a year. The post office did not resume overseas postal service until the first of January, 1947. I waited for Fred to write me first. However, my grandmother kept after me to write him a letter, encouraging me not to wait. She helped me compose a letter. She was very supportive. We drafted a letter carefully since it had been a long time since he left Germany, and I didn't want him to feel obligated to keep his promises in case he married someone else. In the letter, I asked how he was and if he made it home safely. By then, our street address had changed also. I sealed the letter and sent it to his parents' address, ensuring that it had our new return address. Letters took several weeks to cross the Atlantic, and I waited for his reply.

Ecstatic to receive my letter with our new address, he went immediately to the Consulate to begin processing the papers needed to bring me to the United States to get married. Eventually he told me that he didn't write to me first, because the address I had given him would most likely be blocked by the U.S Post Master, and I wouldn't have received it. Our street address he had when he left Germany was on, "Adolf Hitler Street!" He felt that sending mail to that address would cause an inquiry, or probe into his activities by the U.S. government. During WWII the FBI detained his father in an internment camp as an "alien enemy" based on his German decent, so he decided to be cautious and wait until all restrictions were lifted.

A letter took three or four weeks to cross overseas. I received his first letter around the first week of March 1947. My hands shook as I opened it. His first words read, "If you still want to marry me, fill out these papers." So, I did!

It took several months to apply for a passport and visa while the government did an investigation on me first. The military police (MPs) questioned people in my neighborhood about my political views, social activities, and acquaintances. Our neighbor came over and told us that an MP asked him if he knew me, and if he would answer questions about me. He agreed, and the MP asked, "How many soldiers came over to the house?"

"Only one soldier came over there named Fred," he answered. "I was there when Fred met Leni, and I knew then that they were in love. If that wasn't love at first sight then I don't know what is!" he said.

Once the investigation was completed I was notified by the Consulate that my papers were ready. Fred thought it would take a month to process my papers, but it took much longer. When all of the paper work was in order, I received my passport and visa in July 1947.

The Red Cross kept Fred informed of the progress. Fred had to put down $200 for my trip to America, as well as a note deposited for $500 in case we did not get married by the end of three months, at which point I would have to return to Germany.

I went to Duisburg to say farewell to my relatives and cousins before I left for America. I decided to visit the Gesenhaus family in Walsum and give them the letters and drawings I saved from Franz during the war as a gesture of goodwill. Mrs. Gesenhaus, a

My Kennkarte (Identification) card.

devout Roman Catholic, was grateful, but asked me a personal question about Franz before I left.

"When you were alone with my son in the field during his last furlough, did he have sex with you?"

"No!" I answered truthfully. "We sat in the grass talking and he was a gentleman," I said.

She looked relieved, and made the sign of the cross, and she blessed me, saying that she hoped I would have a good life in America.

CHAPTER 23

I Leave for America

My father and mother were sad to see me go, especially since I was their only child and they had never met Fred. But they gave me their blessings and were truly happy for me. I was now twenty-three years old and ready to live my own life.

My father constructed a trunk for me to pack my clothes into for the journey to America. One afternoon, I heard him working on it in the back room and I looked around the door. He didn't see me, but I saw tears running down his face as he tapped on a nail with his hammer. It was the first time I ever saw him cry. I stepped away finally realizing how difficult it must have been for my parents to let me go. They would not be able to give me a wedding reception they dreamed of, they would not be able to see me in a wedding dress as I walked down the wedding aisle, nor would they meet Fred. A wave of emotion swept through me, one of emptiness and uncertainty. "Have I made the right choice?" I thought. Then I sighed, and I knew that I had.

I had to stay at a camp in Bremen for two weeks prior to my departure to America. Once I checked in, I couldn't leave the camp. My parents were told that they could visit with me the day before departure. Only two of us were going to America to get married. Most people were refugees held in concentration camps during the war. My parents did come back to the camp to see me

I came to America on the Marine Flasher.
Photo courtesy U.S. Maritime Commission.

for the last time before I left. I tried to be strong and jokingly said, "I will either see you in three months or twenty years."

Officials escorted us to our ship, the S.S. Marine Flasher. It was a C4 type troopship that provided passage for many Holocaust survivors and people trying to build a new life in the USA after WWII. The ship departed on July 24th, 1947.

The American Consulate sent Fred a Western Union telegram, notifying him that I departed. My parents were told which pier my ship would be leaving from, but for some reason they went to the wrong pier and I didn't get to wave good-bye to them. The shore was crowded with so many people. I looked for them, but I never saw them. Later in a letter, they wrote that they saw my ship when it left, but they couldn't reach me in time. I was heartbroken, and I know that they were too. Maybe it was for the best that I didn't see them; I might have changed my mind. Regardless, I waved with the crowd, hoping that they saw me.

The sleeping quarters were below deck, filled with bunk beds. There was a cafeteria on board as well, and I saw that each table had a bowl of fruit and appetizers on it. I reached down and took a couple of plums. I was very hungry and I took a bite of one and spit it out thinking it was a rotten plum! I tried tasting the other one and it was repugnant also. I never tasted one again, but later learned that they were large black olives, not plums.

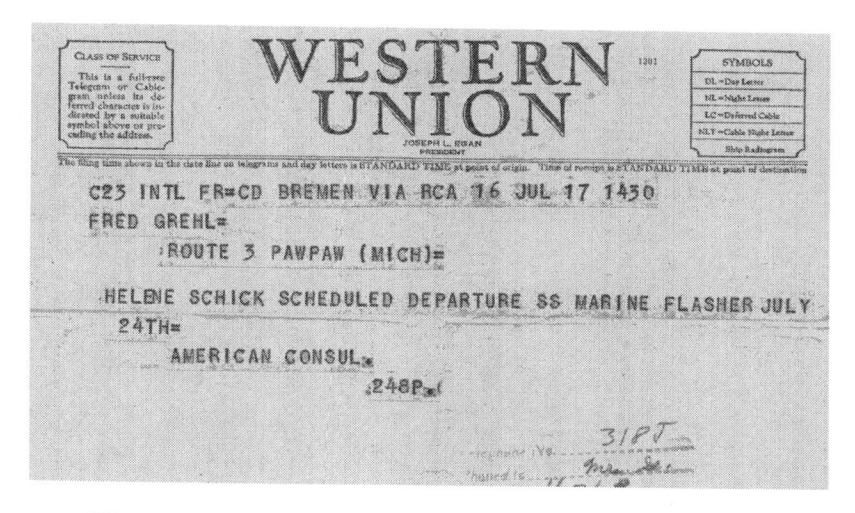

The American Consulate sent a telegram to Fred when I departed Bremen on July 24, 1947.

I spent most of my time on the first deck floor. Sitting on the floor helped prevent me from getting seasick. We could feel the ship rock more heavily down in the sleeping quarters. One night, we sailed through a large storm that violently tossed us around. Our sleeping quarters were right above the engine room. That same night, the engines suddenly stopped, and it was quiet. This was a strange feeling after being accustomed to the noise. The motors broke and were not fixed until the morning. This made us a day late to port, taking ten days instead of nine.

I met a woman on the ship who was from America but got stranded in Germany when the war broke out. Now, she was returning home. I told her that I was a hairdresser in Germany and that I was going to get married in America. Two days before we were scheduled to arrive at port, she asked me if I would help fix her hair. I styled it and afterwards she reached into her purse and gave me a silver dollar.

She said to me, "Here is a silver dollar. Don't spend it. As long as you have a dollar in your pocket, you will never be broke." I kept it and have never spent that dollar.

Before arriving to port in New York City, I saw the magnificent view of the Statue of Liberty in the distance. Our ship docked in the evening. We stayed on board and around 3:00 a.m. they served us breakfast. Before I got off of the ship, the Captain called me to his office. He had a letter from Fred with money in it. In the letter Fred wrote to use the money for a comfortable Pullman car to sleep in. The Captain told me that Fred would be picking me up at the Kalamazoo train station in Michigan. He said I had enough money for my journey.

People were leaving the ship and lining up at the tables set up on the pier to get directions and help from the Red Cross. As luggage was loaded onto the docks, people had to claim their belongings. I needed to retrieve the trunk that my father made me. It was on the dock, but no one spoke German to help me out. I stood in line at the tables, but they turned me away like it wasn't my turn. So, I just sat by myself all day. By noon, I was still there. Most of the people were helped except for me. Some of the tables were being packed up. I had nowhere to sit so I plopped down on my suitcase. The longer I sat, the more desperate I felt. I had to go to the bathroom; I was hungry, thirsty, and frightfully scared without anyone to turn to for help. I didn't want to leave the pier because I had heard so many stories about gangsters in New York City. I didn't talk to anyone. Before I knew it, there were less and less people there. I was so lonely sitting on my suitcase and it was around 3:00 p.m. by then. I became so upset I started balling. I felt so lost! I was just about ready to get back on the ship, but I kept telling myself, "I have Fred's letter in my hand and he is going to pick me up in Kalamazoo." I could barely keep my courage up when suddenly there was a tap on my shoulder. I glanced up at a lady and she started speaking to me. While I was still crying I said, "Don't speak English" to her. It was a lady from the Red Cross. She tried to comfort me and consoled me in German. She was kind and helpful and took me to a restroom first. She got me a glass of water to drink; she worried I would have a heat stroke wearing a heavy suit on a hot summer day. She looked at my papers to see where I was going.

"The first thing we are going to do is get a taxicab. I am going to take you to the train station," she said. She checked my train schedule and how much money I had, then told the taxi driver to show me around New York City.

I was very excited to see the city and the Empire State Building. I had never seen so much traffic before without a traffic guard. In Germany, a police officer would stand in the center of an intersection directing the traffic. However, here in America the drivers took turns, stopping at the intersections and letting traffic through. They seemed to take turns; I thought the Americans were very courteous! I made a remark about this to the lady from the Red Cross and she laughed and pointed out the streetlights on each corner to me. I had never seen streetlights before and found it amazing.

The taxi dropped us off at Grand Central Station. I was overwhelmed by its largeness. The lady from the Red Cross purchased my train ticket with the money Fred sent me. The station was filled with cart vendors selling candy, chocolate, cookies, and food. I asked her if I could buy something to eat.

The first thing she did was to pull out some change from her pocket and tell me what each coin represented.

"This is a penny. This is a nickel. This is a dime. Remember, that a dime is smaller than a nickel, but is more money." Then she showed me a quarter and told me that it was worth two dimes and a nickel.

"Do you remember?" she asked.

Once she finished with her short lessen on American currency she led me to the cafeteria. I stood in line and ordered bacon, eggs, and bread. She helped me pay for my meal with my own money, and we sat down at a table to eat. I was very hungry and she watched me eat. The German custom is to hold your fork in your left hand and push the food onto it with your knife placed in your right hand.

"If you don't want to look like you just stepped off the boat, then you need to learn to eat the American way," she instructed. "Here in America, you hold your fork in your left hand and your knife in your right hand to cut your food. You switch the fork back to your right hand to eat and put the knife down on the side of the plate," she explained as I watched her.

Then she mentioned that I should push my food onto my fork with my bread, as if I wasn't already perplexed. However, I was amused and I learned "her" way, and never forgot those first lessons in American manners.

My train was scheduled to depart around 5:30 p.m. The lady from the Red Cross escorted me to the train and spoke with the conductor to ensure that I did not get off of the train until they reached Kalamazoo, Michigan. She told him that my ticket was for a Pullman and asked him if he would show me where my seat was located. I gave her a hug good-bye. She said she would call Fred and let him know that I made it to the train and that I should arrive in Kalamazoo around 10:30 a.m. the next morning, August fourth.

After they seated me, a lady sat across the aisle from me. The Pullman car turned into a bed at night, and I had that whole compartment to myself. My compartment was close to the kitchen and the waiters began serving food. My waiter had just walked from the kitchen when the train suddenly jerked and his platter of food crashed down right in front of my feet! I was so startled that the lady sitting across the aisle motioned for me to sit next to her while they cleaned up the mess. She started to talk to me, but I couldn't understand her. I remembered that I had a book with me that translated German into English. I took it out and we both were looking through it trying to find words to have some kind of conversation with each other. We had so much fun pointing at words and giggling at each other's charades that the time passed quickly. I discovered that she took this train ride once a month and was very well acquainted with the kitchen help and the cook. She gave me a tour of the train, the kitchen, and dining car. Before I went to sleep she asked me if I wanted her to wake me up in the morning for breakfast, since she would be getting up early. Her stop was before mine and she wanted me to see a view of a bridge that crossed over into Canada just before her stop. I agreed, and we said goodnight.

As I settled down to sleep in the Pullman, thoughts of uncertainty and doubt haunted my mind as I wondered if I had made the right decision to marry Fred. I felt jittery inside and worried. Nearly two years had passed since we saw each other, and his feelings might have changed in that time. I turned over on my side and tried to remember his face and his tender voice as I drifted off to sleep in anticipation of our reunion the next day.

In the morning, my friend on the train woke me and we had breakfast together. I showed her Fred's letter and she checked to see where I was going because she didn't understand how I pronounced it. I didn't pronounce Paw Paw and Kalamazoo correctly. I said, "Puff Puff" and "Ka-la-mat-zu." She said, "No! It is Kal-la-ma-zoo and P-aw P-aw!" Before she got off the train she told the conductor I was departing at Kalamazoo. He kept an eye on me. Once I almost got off at the wrong stop, but he grabbed me by the collar and shook his head.

Finally, the whistle blew and the conductor announced, "Next stop Kalamazoo!" Fred was waiting there with his family. I anxiously stood up and my heart began to race with excitement to see him again. I waited at the door threshold in anticipation for the train to stop. I saw his smiling face and a sparkle of love in his eyes, and I knew that nothing had changed between us. I stepped down and he swept me into his arms, kissing and holding me with a passion only lovers know.

The Red Cross was waiting at the train station too. They had me sign papers, showing that I arrived safely. Fred also had to sign that he picked me up.

His family was anxious to meet me, so we didn't speak much. When I saw his sisters, I thought Wilgard was Gisela because she was taller than her sisters. Fred always called Wilgard his "baby sister" so I expected her to be a child. Yet, she was now thirteen years old and very lanky.

Fred's parents hugged me and welcomed me to America. They spoke fluent German and made me feel accepted and loved the moment we met. I was so happy to finally meet Fred's family, and they made me feel like I was part of the family.

They drove home in their car and I rode with Fred in his. While we sat in his car he proposed to me and gave me my engagement ring. I took off the wedding band that Oma gave us and he put his engagement ring on my finger. It wasn't a diamond, because he couldn't afford one after spending all of his money to get me to America. But, it was beautiful to me. We drove through the country on US 12 to Paw Paw where we would live. I had never seen so much open land between towns before and I wondered where he was taking me!

Fred's parents, Fritz and Erna Grehl, owned a restaurant called the Bungalow in Paw Paw. They served home-style food for lunch and dinner. They lived in an apartment in the back of the restaurant. When Fred and I arrived at the restaurant, Fritz and Erna's friends and relatives greeted us. Like Fred's parents, his entire family spoke German; I felt at home around them.

The first thing Gisela did was go into Betty's closet to get me a sundress and shoes to wear. She probably felt sorry for me because I was wearing a heavy suit and it was very hot. She had me take a bath to clean up from my trip. Afterwards, she came into the bathroom with a razor in her hand.

"Leni, you won't need nylons in this heat if your legs are smoothly shaved," she said. "Women in America shave their legs and armpits regularly, and I will show you how," she insisted. (In Germany at that time it was not customary for women to shave.) I just sat there like a puppet on a string while she pulled up my arms and shaved under them and then stretched out my legs to shave them. All I could think to myself was, "Where is she going to shave me next!"

After I bathed and dressed comfortably in a white sundress, Fred drove me around the Village of Paw Paw. It was a small town with a man-made lake in the middle of town called Maple Lake. He took me to Maple Island at the lake to have some time alone together. I took along a bathing suit I borrowed and changed into it inside a public restroom. We sat on a blanket at the waters edge to talk about getting married. We were so happy together and our romance reignited as if we had never been apart.

The next day he took me to Kalamazoo with his sisters to get some new clothes. It was a very hot summer and I didn't have any

I wore Betty Grehl's sundress the first day I arrived to America, August 4, 1947.

summer clothes. His sisters helped me pick out a few outfits. They took me to all of the stores in downtown Kalamazoo, and I tried on lots of clothes. It was August and the stores were having their summer sales with good bargains.

Our wedding date was set for August 18th. Fred's family asked me what kind of wedding we would like to have. I knew that Fred didn't have much money in the bank, so I mentioned that I would be happy with a small wedding. I just wanted to wear a white wedding dress, even if it was borrowed, so that I could send pictures of our wedding to my mother. That was all I had to say! Erna and Fritz helped arrange our wedding and paid for my gown and the bridesmaid dresses for Fred's sisters to be in the wedding. The entire family became involved and ordered the invitations, planned the entrées, cake and reception. They planned and arranged every detail to give us a dream wedding.

One of Fritz and Erna's customers, Mrs. Haars, wanted to give me a wedding shower. Mr. and Mrs. Haars owned a fruit farm, and they had a roadside stand to sell their fresh produce, apple cider, apple juice, peaches, apples, cherries, and pears that were in season. Fred occasionally drove a delivery truck for them to make a few dollars.

Before I went to the shower, the girls were coaching me to say, "It's pretty," "Beautiful," and, "Thank you." When I said it wrong they would correct me. "Thhh-ank you. Not Tank you," I was reminded. On the day of my shower, Fred told me that all I needed to do was just smile and that was enough.

Fred's mother had a shower for me too at the Bungalow. She invited friends from their church and close relatives. They knew that we didn't have anything so we primarily received household items and dishes.

CHAPTER 24

Our Wedding Day

Our wedding was held at the First Presbyterian Church in Paw Paw on August 18, 1947. Fred's sisters, Wilgard and Betty were my bridesmaids, and Gisela was my maid of honor. Fred's best man was his close friend, Bob Sitter. His cousins, Dick Brill and Bobby Brill, served as ushers.

At the wedding rehearsal, the Pastor recited the wedding ceremony to us while Fred interpreted the words for me, so that I would understand the meaning of our vows. The Pastor was very cordial and explained that he would nod his head at me when it was time for me to answer the question: "Do you take this man to be your lawful wedded husband?" with, "yes."

It was a beautiful wedding, held at 4:00 p.m. on the hottest day of the year—reaching 100 degrees! During the wedding ceremony, Fred placed Oma's wedding band on my ring finger as he asked me to be his wife. We had a photographer for the wedding. Unfortunately, only a few of our photos turned out, and we had to touch up those.

Our reception was held at the Gateway Inn Restaurant on US 12 in Paw Paw. Fred's Uncle Harold Brill and Aunt Hilda Brill owned the restaurant. Fred's parents bought the food for the reception, but it was prepared and served by the staff at the restaurant as a gift from the Brill family. The restaurant was beautifully decorated with flowers and centerpieces at each table.

Fred's sisters were our bridesmaids. From the left to right is: Wilgard, Betty, Gisela, Leni, Fred, Bob Sitter, Bob Brill, and Dick Brill.

Uncle Harold had a license to sell wine and beer, but not hard liquor. Fritz bought some liquor and set up a bar outside on the back of his station wagon in the back yard.

After the reception, Fred drove me to Chicago, Illinois in his new car for our honeymoon. We stayed with his Aunty Ann and Uncle Dan Wetzel, whom he was very close to growing up in Chicago. Fred's family lived with them when he was born – only a few days after they immigrated to America in 1923. They lived with them again when they returned from Germany in 1937. His Aunty Ann (Anna Wetzel) was his mother's eldest sister.

During our visit, Fred took me to the Chicago O'Hare Airport to show me the planes flying in and taking off. He also took me to the Chicago Zoo, because I had never seen one. It had exhibits of every species of tropical birds and animals, which made it difficult to see them all in one day.

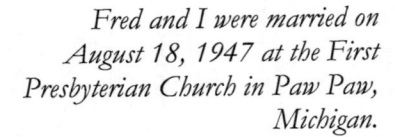

Fred and I were married on August 18, 1947 at the First Presbyterian Church in Paw Paw, Michigan.

Aunty Ann gave us a wedding shower too. Fred's cousins Donny and Audrey Wetzel came to the shower, including some of Aunty Ann's German speaking friends. Between all of the showers and wedding gifts we received, we had a surplus of coffee pots! Fred was hoping more for money than presents, since we really could have used the money for a down payment on a house. However, we also needed items to put in the house.

We drove back with our gifts and stored them in the basement of the Bungalow until construction of the house we wanted to buy was complete. Since we did not receive much money for our wedding, Fred had to make a big decision in order to purchase the house.

CHAPTER 25

Our First House

Fred sold his new Ford Sedan to put a down payment on a house under construction on Liberty Street. It was in Paw Paw, next door to his sister, Gisela's house. It was a charming two-bedroom Cape Cod style house, painted white. He made $700 selling his car, giving us the amount needed for the down payment, plus some extra to buy some furniture for the house. He originally ordered the car from the automobile factory after the war, and it took months to get it. He made a profit when he sold it, because the buyer was willing to pay more in order to take it right away. He purchased it on the spot, leaving us without any vehicle for transportation. The house wasn't ready until September, so we stayed in the basement of the Bungalow. We moved into the house on September 6th, 1947.

Two weeks before I arrived to America, Fred was laid off from his manufacturing job at Eaton's in Lawton. He did not want to look for another job right away because he figured he wouldn't get time off if he started at a new job. When we got back from our honeymoon in Chicago he started looking for new work. Here we were just married, purchasing a new house and new furniture, without a job or a car!

He walked everyday to US 12, the nearest highway, to hitchhike into Kalamazoo to apply for work. Then one morning as he stood waiting by the highway for a ride, he noticed that the

State Highway Department was open across the street and he decided to ask if they were hiring. They hired him on the spot, and he returned home to tell me the good news.

"What are you doing home so soon?" I asked.

"I got a job at the State Highway Department!" he said with a grin he couldn't contain. It was the stroke of good luck that we were hoping for as we began our new life together.

He walked to the State Highway Department, only a few blocks away, each day to work. It was several months before we could purchase another car.

I was home alone while he worked long hours and weekends most of the time. During this period, I became homesick. Up until then, we were busy planning the wedding, buying a house, moving, and settling into a daily routine; I never had time to get homesick. Fred's sister, Gisela Sullivan lived next door to us and I confided in her. I don't know what I would have done without her companionship. We kept each other company, and I saw her everyday. I was very fortunate to have a German speaking family around me, although Gisela's husband, Jimmy could not speak German.

I was in America about four months when Jimmy interrupted a German conversation between Gisela and me.

"Isn't it about time *she* learns how to speak English?" he snapped at Gisela. "If she wants to be accepted in this country then she should learn the language!" he insisted. Gisela interpreted what he said to me, but I felt hurt and went home. After thinking it over, I realized that he was right, and I asked Fred and his family to help me learn English. Everyone agreed, and I began practicing, but it was not easy.

Gisela and Jimmy had two children, Jamie and Terry, who I babysat. Jamie was very smart and helpful for a girl of four, and

Terry was a cuddly three year old who loved to sit on my lap while I attempted to read children books to him in English. I did not know what I was reading, but I did my best to sound out each word. He didn't care how the words were annunciated, but it must have sounded very funny to Jamie because she distorted her face with every word I read. Terry enjoyed every moment and we played word games together. "What is this?" I asked as I pointed to his ear. "Err," he said, and I repeated it back to him. He carried a favorite towel with him when he took a nap and called it his "taugh taugh." Before long, I became very proficient in the art of speaking English baby talk!

CHAPTER 26

My Father's New Business

In late 1947, shortly after I came to America, the banks and money exchange in Germany opened. I had signed over my savings account to my parents before I left Germany. It was my entire savings I had made as a hairdresser. However, it wasn't worth much any more, maybe 10 cents on the dollar.

I received a letter from my parents telling me about my father's new business venture he started with the money I left them in Germany.

My father had some ideas for starting a small business door-to-door. He decided to withdraw some money from the bank to buy simple commodities he could resell for a small profit. He went to a warehouse to buy thread, needles, buttons, and small items that every household family needed. He sold those items by going house to house on his bicycle each day; always reinvesting his profit. He was very successful and realized that there was a high demand for small commodities. He reinvested his small profit each day and began to build a larger inventory. He eventually became a cart vendor at the Bremen marketplace a few times a week. It worked out so well, he didn't need to sell door-to-door anymore.

My father met with a cousin on my mother's side that owned a butcher shop and a vacant lot. They agreed that Johann could rent

My father owned and operated a small convenient store in Bremen, Germany after the war.

a space on his lot to build a small convenience store. He sold school supplies, paper, pencils, soda, and penny candy to the local children walking by each day to school. His business flourished and he soon began to sell food, and also chocolates and candies for the holidays. Later, he expanded his store and sold beer and cigarettes. He added an area in the back for storage and a room for a table and chairs. He bought a two-burner gas stove to cook himself lunch during the day so he wouldn't have to leave the store. My parents made a new start in life for themselves after the war, and I was happy for them.

Every year my father sent me money for Christmas in German currency that we exchanged into U. S. dollars to buy Christmas gifts. He packed and shipped a large carton of assorted German chocolates and candy for us each year that we shared with Fred's parents and friends during the holidays. We were very excited when the package arrived, as it contained varieties of brandy-filled chocolates and fillings that Fred and I relished.

CHAPTER 27

Starting a Family

On September 2, 1948, I gave birth to a beautiful baby girl. We named her Linda and she had beautiful brown curls so I called her my little Shirley Temple.

I was beginning to get a good grasp of the English language when Linda was a baby, but some words and phrases did not translate well from German to English. When I took Linda to the doctor for a checkup, Dr. Tenhouten asked me if I had any questions for him.

"Can you clean Linda's ears?" I asked. "She seems to have a lot of lard in them," I added.

In a humorous smirk he asked, "How did she get *lard* in her ears?" Then, struggling to keep a straight face he said, "I think you meant *wax* in her ears," and he chuckled again at my translation.

Fred was a wonderful husband and father, and he hoped that our next child would be a boy. By 1950 I was expecting again, but this time we learned that there was more than one. During my pre-natal examination he listened carefully through his stethoscope and discovered a second heartbeat.

"You are pregnant with twins!" he exclaimed.

Fred and I were elated, but I was afraid to tell my mother the news, knowing that she would be worried and anxious about me being so far away. Late in my pregnancy, I finally wrote to her and

Fred is holding Linda on her first Christmas at three months old.

told her I was expecting again, but I kept the news of carrying twins from her.

Over the next several months we prepared for the twins' arrival, but we never prepared for the unexpected news we received in the mailbox. While I was pregnant in the last trimester with the twins, we received an unexpected notice from the government to repay a GI grant given to Fred in 1946 for the amount of $3,000. Fred was devastated. When he returned from the war he finished his high school education, and then applied for a GI grant to attend Western University in Kalamazoo. He went to college the first year, but he didn't have a car to drive and he had to hitchhike to Kalamazoo to go to classes. He eventually had to quit school because it was too difficult to get there. He contacted the administration to notify them that he could not finish his education and to stop sending the grant money. Yet, they continued to send him monthly checks and he cashed them. He didn't realize that he could be penalized for using that money for things other than for college. The checks eventually stopped coming without any notice. When his car was delivered from the factory, he paid for it with his grant money. After a couple of years he had forgotten about the GI grant until the notice appeared in our mailbox.

Fritz, Fred's father, sold the Bungalow and Fred asked him if he could borrow money from him to repay the government. But Fritz couldn't loan it to him because he and Erna were preparing to go to Germany for several months. Fred requested to have a meeting with the debt collectors to review his case. He frantically told them that we did not have the money right now and that we were expecting twins. He just started work again at Eaton's in Lawton and he asked them if he could pay it back monthly. They reduced the amount he had to pay down to $1,500 dollars. Even though they reduced it, he had to pay it back in full. Fred was so desperate that he went to his friend Jake Freego and asked him if he would loan us the money. He owned a farm and was a good friend. Without hesitation, Jake gave it to him. We paid our debt to the government and learned a hard lesson. We made monthly payments to Jake and paid back every penny we owed him, never forgetting his generosity.

On March 26, 1951, I gave birth to healthy twins: a boy and a girl. We named them Raymond and Rita. Raymond weighed seven pounds at birth, while Rita weighed only three pounds. After their births, I wrote my mother another letter to tell her. "Remember when I wrote you that Linda was going to have a baby brother or a sister? Well, Linda got a brother and a sister!"

We now had our hands busy with three children. My mother was diagnosed with uterine cancer and saddened that she had never seen her grandchildren except in pictures, nor had she ever met Fred. By 1953 she came to America by herself and stayed with

*The twins,
Rita and Raymond
one year old.*

us for a few months while my father attended to his store. It was one of the happiest times together we ever had, yet one of the most difficult times to face when she had to return to Germany.

My parents continued to live with my grandparents in Aumund through 1955. My mother died of cancer on November 11, 1955. Shortly afterwards, my father moved into a new apartment he had waited for since the end of the war. He was able to get a pension as a disabled veteran from WWI. He needed a caretaker and met a woman named Erna. She took care of him, helped him in his store, and eventually became his second wife.

Each year my father continued to send us a Christmas package of chocolates and gifts to delight the family. As the children grew older they sat around us anxiously watching to see what was inside it for them. I pulled out boxes of chocolate candies and chocolate bars in every variety of flavors and fillings to last us a lifetime it seemed. Rich assortments of caramels, truffles, marzipan, and brandy liqueur were separated out onto the floor; while eager eyes

From the left is my father, Johann Schick, Erna Grehl, Erna Schick, and Fritz Grehl visiting in Bremen, Germany in the early 60's.

marveled at the treasure of candy before them. He sent a mixture of everything, including kinder schokolade (children chocolate), with chocolate foil-wrapped Santas, reindeer, and bells for the Christmas holiday. The children relished those treats every year.

Me standing next to Fred's 1946 Ford sedan he sold to buy our house.

I am holding Linda in front of our house in the spring of 1949.

My mother and I, Christmas 1952.

Auguste Diemer (Little Oma) holding Linda a few weeks old.

Love, War & Curling Irons 133

Rita and Linda.

Ray, Rita and Linda at Easter.

Family picture at the Gateway Inn.

Linda 3 years old.

My mother and I with the kids 1952.

CHAPTER 28

The American Dream

Life in Paw Paw took on a sense of normalcy once the twins could walk and I could speak English more fluently. We now owned a car, Fred worked at Eaton's in Lawton, and we had a dog named Girlie. Life in a small community was a perfect setting for raising our young family, and we were happily living the American dream.

I sought American citizenship in 1952. I applied at the Van Buren County Court House and had to pass the U.S. Citizenship Test before the ceremony date was granted. On Friday, November 21, 1952, I proudly pledged my oath of citizenship and became an official U.S. citizen.

Once Ray and Rita were five years old and ready to start kindergarten, I thought about going back to beauty school to become licensed in America. Fred took me to Kalamazoo to a cosmetology school to inquire about it. After explaining my background in Germany and showing them my certifications, they decided to let me work in their beauty salon under the guidance of the teacher to learn the salons products and American names for them. I rode a bus to Kalamazoo to get to the salon each day. The bus stopped at the Greyhound station, where I got off and walked to the salon. It was difficult to schedule my clients' appointments around the bus schedule, so after I got my license, I applied at salons in Paw Paw. I was hired at Audrey's Beauty Salon downtown and worked with Audrey Jacobs and Juanita Ball.

It was then that I felt I belonged to this country, fulfilling my purpose in life. The homesickness for Germany subsided as I now devoted all of my love and attention to Fred, our children, our home, and my new career in America. It provided our family an additional income, but more importantly, a position with some flexibility I needed while raising three energetic children. We remained in the same town and quaint house on Liberty Street, remodeling and expanding the kitchen and dinning area, including an additional bedroom to accommodate our growing family in 1960.

Then in December of 1966, approximately twenty years after I left Germany, I returned home to visit my father and relatives in Bremen-Vegasack as I promised my parents twenty years earlier before I boarded the S.S. Marine Flasher. I saw my father one more time in 1969 when my daughter Rita and I traveled to Germany for the Christmas season. He lived until May 3, 1971.

Our children grew up to become successful individuals in their own career choices and then married with beautiful children of their own. We became proud grandparents of eight grandchildren named: Andrea, Brian, Sarah, Eric, Kayla, Heather, John, and April.

After thirty years, Fred was forced to retire from Eaton's Fuller Transmission Division in Kalamazoo when the company closed in October 1981. It was then that I decided to retire from Audrey's Beauty Salon after twenty-five years. We put our house up for sale and traveled west looking at areas to move to for our retirement. During our travels, we drove through Carlsbad, New Mexico and instantly felt a connection when we met wonderful people from the senior center. We picked up a local newspaper

Fred and I overlooking the city of Carlsbad, New Mexico in 2002.

and inquired about a very affordable, fully furnished duplex for rent and to our surprise it was available immediately. We moved in and began our retirement in Carlsbad in November 1981. After our house in Michigan sold, we bought a house in Carlsbad at 203 S. Elm Street and lived there for a period of twenty-five years.

During our retirement we enjoyed traveling. We traveled by car to see the many beautiful sights of our country and visited our children and grandchildren each year. We became great-grandparents of five great-grandchildren named: Tara, Evan, Haley, Travis, and Fred (named after his great-grandfather Fred).

Fred enjoyed golfing and I enjoyed oil painting. We went to the senior center on Wednesday and Friday evenings for dance night. The band played all of the old big band songs that we knew since the 40s when Fred and I first met. Even at the age of eighty, we still danced to swing music, the jitterbug, and even the twist together. But what we enjoyed most of all was dancing cheek-to-cheek, stirring the same feelings of romance we always felt for each other since our first dance together long ago.

ISBN 142518653-X

Made in the USA
Middletown, DE
09 June 2016